As a study abroad consultant, I understand the importance of accurate and reliable information for those seeking to embark on an international educational journey.

This publication has been carefully crafted to provide just that. It is important to note, however, that this book is not intended to replace any professional advice or services.

While it is our goal to provide the most up-to-date and comprehensive information possible, the author and publisher are not engaged in rendering any psychological services.

Therefore, we strongly encourage our readers to seek out the guidance of professionals as needed throughout their study abroad experience. With this in mind, we hope that this book serves as a valuable resource to aid in your journey toward academic and personal growth.

TABLE OF CONTENTS

About Study Metro

Study Metro is a platform that connects universities and students for studying abroad. We offer one-stop solutions, allowing students to apply directly to 12,000+ universities and 500k+ study abroad programs.

We facilitate seamless communication between universities and students, discussing admission requirements and scholarships. Our platform offers direct access to service providers like trainers, education loan providers, writers, forex, and travel agents. agents can work with us for high commissions. We provide an information center for parents and virtual events for students.

Lastly, we share student profiles with universities to onboard them for undergraduate or graduate programs with the highest scholarships available.

For More Infomation:
Visit: **www.studymetro.com**
Call: **+91 7898 23 6622**

About Author

Abhishek Bajaj is a visionary leader in the field of education abroad. As the co-founder and managing director of Study Metro, Mr. Bajaj has dedicated his career to making education abroad accessible and affordable to students worldwide.

With over 16 years of experience in the technology and study abroad education industry, Mr. Bajaj has become a driving force in transforming the sector into something more progressive. His technical expertise has allowed him to simplify the complex counseling and application process into easy-to-follow steps for students, making the application process simpler and easier.

Mr. Bajaj's commitment to innovation has also led him to develop a SAAS-based platform for easy operation and application processing for students and universities. By creating a marketplace for all study abroad education providers to meet students in one place, he has revolutionized the industry and made it easier for students to access the education they desire.

Before co-founding Study Metro, Mr. Bajaj worked as a System Administrator with HSBC Global Technologies (INDIA) ltd Hyderabad, and as an AIX Specialist with Gulf Business Machines (GBM) Qatar. He received his Bachelor's in Computer Science from Rajiv Gandhi Prodyogiki Vishwavidyalaya, Bhopal.

Mr. Bajaj is a certified member of the American International Council and an active member of NAFSA since 2017. Through his leadership, Mr. Bajaj has been able to establish Study Metro as a trusted and respected brand in the study abroad education industry. With his passion and dedication, he has helped countless students achieve their dreams of studying abroad.

Acknowledgement

Writing a book is never a solitary effort, and this book on **"Exploring Study Abroad Opportunities After 12th"** is no exception. It is with great pleasure that I extend my heartfelt thanks to all those who have contributed to this book and made it possible.

First and foremost, I would like to express my gratitude to the students who have inspired me to write this book. Your eagerness to explore study abroad opportunities after the 12th and your enthusiasm to learn more about it have been the driving force behind this project.

I am indebted to my family for their unwavering support throughout the writing process. Their encouragement and understanding have kept me motivated and focused on completing this book.

I would also like to acknowledge the many educators, professionals, and organizations that generously shared their knowledge and expertise on the subject. Your contributions have enriched the content of this book and will undoubtedly help students make informed decisions about studying abroad.

Lastly, I am grateful to the team at the publishing house who helped bring this book to fruition. Their professionalism, expertise, and support have been invaluable.

In conclusion, this book would not have been possible without the support of so many individuals and organizations. I extend my heartfelt thanks to all of you for your contributions and support.

Study Abroad: Introduction

Studying abroad is a popular option for students who want to broaden their horizons and gain international experience while pursuing their academic goals. In simple terms, study abroad refers to a program in which a student enrolls in an educational institution outside their home country to complete part or all of their degree program.

There are several types of study abroad programs available, ranging from short-term study tours to full degree programs. Short-term programs typically last a few weeks to a few months and involve traveling to a foreign country to participate in courses, cultural activities, and field trips. They are often offered during the summer or winter break and provide students with a chance to experience a new culture and gain international exposure.

On the other hand, full degree programs abroad typically require students to complete a significant portion of their degree in a foreign country. These programs can last anywhere from a semester to a full academic year or more. They provide students with an opportunity to immerse themselves in a foreign culture, gain proficiency in a foreign language, and build a global network of contacts that can be valuable in their future careers.

To participate in a study abroad program, students typically need to apply to a host institution or program provider that offers courses or programs that align with their academic interests and goals.
Some universities and colleges have their study abroad programs, while others work with third-party providers that specialize in arranging study abroad programs for students.

Studying abroad can be an enriching experience, providing students with the opportunity to gain a new perspective on their academic discipline, develop language and cultural skills, and expand their personal and professional networks. It can also be challenging, as students may face culture shock, language barriers, and homesickness, among other challenges. However, with proper preparation and support, studying abroad can be a life-changing experience that can have a positive impact on a student's personal and professional development.

The benefits of studying abroad after 12th

Studying abroad after completing 12th grade can be a life-changing experience for students. It provides them with an opportunity to gain international exposure, develop new skills, and broaden their horizons. In this article, we will discuss the benefits of studying abroad after 12th.

1. **Exposure to a new culture and lifestyle**

Studying abroad allows students to immerse themselves in a new culture and experience a different way of life. This exposure can broaden their perspectives, expand their knowledge, and improve their understanding of different cultures and ways of thinking.

2. **Opportunity to learn a new language**

Studying abroad provides an excellent opportunity to learn a new language. Learning a new language can enhance communication skills, boost confidence, and improve employability in an increasingly global job market.

3. **Access to high-quality education**

Studying abroad provides access to some of the best educational institutions in the world. These institutions offer a wide range of courses, cutting-edge research facilities, and top-notch faculty. This exposure to a world-class education can be invaluable for students looking to pursue careers in competitive fields.

4. **Career opportunities**

Studying abroad can improve employability and career prospects.

Employers often value candidates who have international experience, as it shows that they have the ability to adapt to new environments and have a global perspective.
Studying abroad can also provide opportunities for internships, work-study programs, and networking with professionals in various industries.

5. Personal development

Studying abroad can be a transformative experience that leads to personal growth and development. Living in a new country can improve independence, self-confidence, and communication skills. It can also help students become more adaptable and resilient, which can be valuable skills in both personal and professional life.

6. Travel opportunities

Studying abroad provides opportunities to travel and explore new places. It can be an excellent opportunity to learn about different cultures, cuisines, and lifestyles. These experiences can also lead to personal growth and broaden perspectives.

In conclusion, studying abroad after completing 12th grade can be a life-changing experience that offers numerous benefits. It provides students with the opportunity to gain international exposure, learn new skills, and broaden their horizons. It can also enhance employability and career prospects while improving personal growth and development.

A. Semester abroad programs

Semester abroad programs are study programs offered by universities and colleges that allow students to spend one or two semesters studying at a partner institution in another country. These programs provide students with an opportunity to experience a new culture, learn a new language, and gain international experience while earning credits toward their degree.

Here are some of the key features of semester-abroad programs:

1. Partner institutions

Semester abroad programs are typically offered through partnerships between universities and colleges. This partnership allows students to take classes at the partner institution and receive credits towards their degree.

2. Length of program

Semester abroad programs typically last for one or two semesters, depending on the institution and the program requirements.

3. Academic credit

One of the key benefits of semester abroad programs is that students can earn academic credits towards their degree. The credits earned abroad can be transferred to their home institution, provided they meet the academic requirements of their home institution.

4. Courses offered

Semester abroad programs offer a wide range of courses, depending on the partner institution and the program requirements.

Students can choose from courses in their major, as well as courses in other disciplines that may not be available at their home institution

5. **Language requirements**
Somesemester abroad programs require students to have a certain level of proficiency in the language of the host country. However, many programs offer language courses or have courses taught in English to accommodate students who do not speak the language of the host country

6.**Housing**
optionsHousing options for semester abroad programs vary depending on the program and the host institution. Some programs offer homestays with local families, while others provide dormitory-style housing or apartments

7.**Cultural activities**
Most semester abroad programs include cultural activities and excursions to help students experience the local culture and make the most of their time abroad. These activities can include city tours, visits to museums, and cultural events.
In conclusion, semester abroad programs are an excellent way for students to gain international experience, learn about new cultures, and earn academic credits towards their degree. These programs offer a wide range of courses, housing options, and cultural activities that can enhance a student's academic and personal growth. If you are considering studying abroad, a semester abroad program may be a great option to explore.

b. Summer programs

Study abroad summer programs are short-term study programs offered by universities and colleges that allow students to spend a summer term studying at a partner institution in another country. These programs provide students with an opportunity to experience a new culture, learn a new language, and gain international experience while earning credits towards their degree.

Here are some of the key features of study abroad summer programs:

1.Short-term program

Study abroad summer programs typically last for 4-8 weeks, depending on the institution and the program requirements. This makes them an ideal option for students who are unable to commit to a full semester abroad.

2.Academic credit

Similar to semester abroad programs, study abroad summer programs allow students to earn academic credits towards their degree. The credits earned abroad can be transferred to their home institution, provided they meet the academic requirements of their home institution

3.Courses offered

Study abroad summer programs offer a range of courses, depending on the partner institution and the program requirements. Students can choose from courses in their major, as well as courses in other disciplines that may not be available at their home institution.

4.Language requirements

Some study abroad summer programs require students to have a certain level of proficiency in the language of the host country. However, many programs offer language courses or have courses taught in English to accommodate students who do not speak the language of the host country

5. Housing options

Housing options for study abroad summer programs vary depending on the program and the host institution. Some programs offer homestays with local families, while others provide dormitory-style housing or apartments.

6.Cultural activities

Most study abroad summer programs include cultural activities and excursions to help students experience the local culture and make the most of their time abroad. These activities can include city tours, visits to museums, and cultural events.

7.Professional development

Study abroad summer programs can also offer professional development opportunities. Many programs offer internships or work-study programs, which can help students gain practical experience in their field of study and improve their employability.

In conclusion, study abroad summer programs are an excellent way for students to gain international experience, learn about new cultures, and earn academic credits towards their degree. These programs offer a range of courses, housing options, and cultural activities that can enhance a student's academic and personal growth. If you are considering studying abroad, a study abroad summer program may be a great option to explore.

.C. Full degree programs

Study abroad full degree programs are study programs offered by universities and colleges that allow students to complete an entire degree program in another country. These programs provide students with an opportunity to experience a new culture, learn a new language, and gain international experience while earning their degree.

Here are some of the key features of study abroad full degree programs:

1. Partner institutions

Study abroad full degree programs are typically offered through partnerships between universities and colleges in different countries. This partnership allows students to complete their degrees at the partner institution and receive a degree from both institutions.

2. Length of program

Study abroad full degree programs typically last for the duration of the degree program, which is usually three to four years for an undergraduate degree and one to two years for a graduate degree.

3. Academic credit

Similar to a semester abroad and summer programs, study abroad full degree programs allow students to earn academic credits towards their degree. The credits earned abroad can be transferred to their home institution, provided they meet the academic requirements of their home institution.

.4. Courses offered study

Abroad full degree programs offer a range of courses, depending on the partner institution and the program requirements.

Students can choose from courses in their major, as well as courses in other disciplines that may not be available at their home institutions.

5. Language requirements

Some study abroad full degree programs require students to have a certain level of proficiency in the language of the host country. However, many programs offer language courses or have courses taught in English to accommodate students who do not speak the language of the host country.

6. Housing options

Housing options for study abroad full degree programs vary depending on the program and the host institution. Some programs offer homestays with local families, while others provide dormitory-style housing or apartments.

7. Cultural

activities Most study abroad full degree programs include cultural activities and excursions to help students experience the local culture and make the most of their time abroad. These activities can include city tours, visits to museums, and cultural events.

In conclusion, study abroad full degree programs are an excellent way for students to gain international experience, learn about new cultures, and earn a degree from a partner institution.

These programs offer a range of courses, housing options, and cultural activities that can enhance a student's academic and personal growth. If you are considering studying abroad, a study abroad full degree program may be a great option to explore. However, it is important to carefully research the program and the partner institution to ensure it is the right fit for your academic and personal goals.

D. Language immersion programs

Language immersion programs for study abroad provide an excellent opportunity for students to enhance their language skills, cultural understanding, and personal growth. These programs typically involve students living and studying in a foreign country where the language they want to learn is spoken. This article will explore the benefits of language immersion programs and provide tips on how to choose the right program.

Benefits of Language Immersion Programs for Study Abroad

1. Enhance Language Skills:

Language immersion programs offer an unparalleled opportunity to improve language skills. Living in a foreign country and interacting with native speakers on a daily basis allows students to quickly pick up on new vocabulary, grammar, and colloquial expressions.

2. Cultural Understanding:

Immersion programs allow students to experience the culture of the country firsthand. They can attend local festivals, visit museums and historical sites, and participate in cultural activities. This firsthand experience provides a deeper understanding of the culture and allows students to appreciate cultural differences.

3. Personal Growth:

Studying abroad is a life-changing experience that can help students develop independence, adaptability, and self-confidence. Living in a foreign country requires students to step out of their comfort zone and navigate unfamiliar situations. This experience can help students become more resilient and adaptable in their personal and professional lives.

4. **Career Advancement:**

Language proficiency and cultural understanding are valuable assets in the global job market. Immersion programs demonstrate to potential employers that students have a deep understanding of the language and culture of a specific country, making them attractive candidates for international positions.

Choosing the Right Language Immersion Program

When choosing a language immersion program, students should consider the following factors:

1. **Location:**

Choose a location that interests you and where the language you want to learn is spoken. Consider the safety of the country and the availability of resources for international students.

2. **Program Type:**

Consider the type of program that best fits your needs. Some programs are designed for beginners, while others are more advanced. Some programs are focused on language learning, while others combine language learning with cultural activities

3. **Program Duration:**

Consider the length of the program and how it fits into your academic schedule. Some programs are designed for a semester, while others are shorter or longer.

4. **Cost:**

Consider the cost of the program and any additional expenses such as airfare, housing, and meals. Look into scholarships or financial aid that may be available to help offset costs.

Conclusion Language immersion programs for study abroad are an excellent way to enhance language skills, cultural understanding, and personal growth.

When choosing a program, consider the location, program type, duration, and cost. With careful planning and preparation, students can have a life-changing experience that will benefit them personally and professionally for years to come.

E. Internship and volunteer programs

Internship and volunteer programs to study abroad provide an excellent opportunity for students to gain real-world experience while immersed in a new culture. These programs typically involve students working with a local organization or company in a foreign country. This article will explore the benefits of internship and volunteer programs and provide tips on how to choose the right program.

Benefits of Internship and Volunteer Programs for Study Abroad

1. Gain Real-World Experience:

Internship and volunteer programs offer an opportunity to gain practical skills and experience in a professional environment. This experience can help students develop their skills and build their resumes, making them more competitive in the job market.

2. Cultural Understanding:

Working with local organizations or companies allows students to gain a deeper understanding of the culture and society of the host country. This experience provides a unique perspective on the culture, and students can learn how cultural differences impact the workplace and daily life.

4. Networking Opportunities:

Internship and volunteer programs offer an opportunity to build professional relationships with local organizations, companies, and professionals. These relationships can be beneficial for future career opportunities or personal connections in the host country

Choosing the Right Internship or Volunteer Program

When choosing an internship or volunteer program, students should consider the following factors:

1. Field of Interest:
Choose a program that aligns with your field of study or career goals. Consider the type of work you would like to do, such as teaching, healthcare, or environmental conservation
.

2. Location:
Choose a location that interests you and where you can gain valuable experience. Consider the safety of the country and the availability of resources for international students
.

3. Program Type:
Consider the type of program that best fits your needs. Some programs are designed for specific fields of study, while others are more general. Some programs offer academic credit, while others do not.

4. Program Duration:
Consider the length of the program and how it fits into your academic schedule. Some programs are designed for a semester, while others are shorter or longer.

5. Cost:
Consider the cost of the program and any additional expenses such as airfare, housing, and meals. Look into scholarships or financial aid that may be available to help offset costs.

Conclusion
Internship and volunteer programs to study abroad provide an excellent opportunity to gain real-world experience, cultural understanding, personal growth, and networking opportunities.

Popular Destinations for Studying Abroad After 12th

A. United States

The United States of America is a popular destination for students from all over the world who want to pursue higher education. With over 4,000 universities and colleges offering a wide range of programs, the USA provides a rich and diverse academic experience. In this article, we'll explore some of the reasons why studying in the USA could be a great choice for you.

Quality Education

The USA has some of the world's best universities and colleges, including Ivy League institutions like Harvard, Yale, and Princeton. The education system in the USA is renowned for its academic rigor, research opportunities, and practical training. US universities and colleges offer cutting-edge facilities, world-class faculty, and a range of programs in diverse fields such as engineering, business, medicine, and social sciences.

Career Opportunities

Studying in the USA can be a great way to boost your career prospects. US universities and colleges have strong industry partnerships, which means that students have access to internships, co-op programs, and job opportunities. Additionally, a US degree is highly valued in the global job market and can open doors to international job opportunities.

Cultural Diversity

The USA is a melting pot of cultures, and studying in the country provides an opportunity to experience this diversity firsthand. International students can learn in a multicultural environment, interact with people from different backgrounds, and gain a global perspective.

This exposure to diverse perspectives can be invaluable for personal growth and development.

Research Opportunities

The USA is a world leader in research and innovation. US universities and colleges are at the forefront of cutting-edge research in fields such as technology, medicine, and science. Studying in the USA provides opportunities to work with top researchers, access state-of-the-art equipment, and participate in groundbreaking research projects.

Personal Development

Studying in the USA can be an excellent opportunity for personal growth and development. Living in a new country, navigating a new culture, and making new friends can be challenging, but it can also be a rewarding experience. Studying in the USA can help you develop skills such as independence, resilience, and adaptability, which can be valuable for your future endeavors.

Language Skills

English is the primary language of instruction in US universities and colleges. Studying in the USA provides an opportunity to immerse yourself in the language, improve your communication skills, and gain fluency in English. This can be a valuable asset for your future career and personal growth

In conclusion, studying in the USA can be an excellent choice for students who want to pursue higher education, boost their career prospects, and gain a global perspective. With its world-class education system, research opportunities, cultural diversity, and personal growth opportunities, the USA is a great destination for international students.

B United Kingdom

The United Kingdom (UK) has long been a popular destination for international students looking to pursue their higher education. With world-renowned universities, a diverse student community, and rich culture, the UK offers a unique and enriching educational experience.

Here are some reasons why studying in the UK is a great choice

Quality Education: The UK has a long-standing reputation for academic excellence, with four universities consistently ranked among the top ten in the world. The teaching and research quality in the UK is world-class, and degrees obtained from UK universities are recognized worldwide.

Broad Range of Courses: The UK offers a wide range of courses and programs to choose from, including traditional academic subjects such as law, medicine, and engineering, as well as newer, interdisciplinary fields such as environmental studies and data science.

Shorter Degree Programs: In comparison to other countries, degree programs in the UK are typically shorter in duration. Most undergraduate degrees take three years to complete, while master's degrees can be completed in one year, reducing the overall cost of education.

Diverse Student Community:

With over 450,000 international students from over 180 countries, the UK has a diverse and welcoming student community. Students from different backgrounds come together, fostering a multicultural environment that encourages cross-cultural learning and communication.

Cultural Enrichment:

The UK has a rich cultural heritage, with museums, galleries, historical landmarks, and events to explore. Studying in the UK offers students the opportunity to experience British culture firsthand, with the added benefit of meeting students from around the world and gaining a global perspective.

Career Opportunities:

The UK is home to many of the world's leading companies, providing students with a wealth of internship and employment opportunities. UK universities have strong links with industry, offering students practical experience and professional networking opportunities.

Language Skills:

English is the language of instruction in UK universities, providing students with the opportunity to improve their English language skills. Fluency in English is a valuable asset in today's global job market, opening up career opportunities around the world.

Financial Support: The UK offers a range of financial support options to international students, including scholarships, bursaries, and grants. UK universities also offer part-time work opportunities, allowing students to earn money while studying.

In conclusion, studying in the UK provides students with a high-quality education, a diverse and welcoming community, and a unique cultural experience. With its world-class universities, a broad range of courses, and professional opportunities, the UK is a top destination for students seeking to further their education and career prospects.

C. Canada

Canada is a vast and diverse country, known for its natural beauty, welcoming culture, and thriving economy. Studying in Canada can be a life-changing experience, as it provides students with access to world-class education, a multicultural society, and abundant opportunities for personal and professional growth. In this article, we will explore the reasons why studying in Canada is an excellent choice for students from all around the world.

1. High-Quality Education System:

Canada is home to some of the best universities in the world, providing high-quality education to students from all around the globe. The Canadian education system is renowned for its rigorous academic standards, innovative teaching methods, and world-class research facilities. Universities in Canada offer a diverse range of programs, from undergraduate to postgraduate degrees in various fields of study, including business, engineering, medicine, and technology.

2. Multicultural Society:

Canada is one of the most diverse countries in the world, with a multicultural society that embraces different cultures, languages, and traditions. Studying in Canada provides students with an opportunity to learn from people of different backgrounds, which can broaden their perspectives and foster cultural understanding. Moreover, Canada is known for its friendly and welcoming culture, which makes it easier for international students to adapt to a new environment and feel at home.

3. Affordable Tuition Fees:

Compared to other English-speaking countries such as the United States, Canada offers affordable tuition fees for international students.

In addition, Canadian universities provide various scholarships and financial aid programs to help students cover their expenses, making it easier for them to pursue their academic dreams.

4. Post-Graduation Work Opportunities:

After completing their studies, international students in Canada have the opportunity to work and gain valuable work experience in their field of study. Canada's post-graduation work permit program allows international students to work in Canada for up to three years after graduation, providing them with an opportunity to gain Canadian work experience and potentially obtain permanent residency.

5. High Quality of Life:

Canada is consistently ranked as one of the best places to live in the world, with a high quality of life, an excellent healthcare system, and safe cities. Studying in Canada provides students with access to a safe and welcoming environment, with opportunities to explore the country's natural beauty, culture, and recreational activities.

In conclusion, studying in Canada provides students with a world-class education, a multicultural society, affordable tuition fees, post-graduation work opportunities, and a high quality of life. These reasons make Canada an excellent destination for international students who want to pursue their academic and professional goals while experiencing a unique cultural and personal growth experience.

D. Australia

Australia has become one of the top choices for international students looking to pursue higher education. With its world-class education system, vibrant culture, and beautiful landscape, Australia has a lot to offer to students. In this article, we will explore some of the reasons why studying in Australia is an excellent choice.

1. Quality Education System

Australia is known for its high-quality education system, with several top-ranked universities consistently ranking among the best in the world. Australian universities offer a wide range of programs, from undergraduate to postgraduate degrees, as well as vocational courses. Additionally, Australian universities have a strong focus on research, making them ideal for students looking to pursue research-based careers.

2. Diverse Culture

Australia is a multicultural country that welcomes people from all around the world. This makes it an excellent place for international students to study and experience different cultures. The country's diverse population provides a unique opportunity to learn about different cultures and customs while making new friends and networking with people from different backgrounds.

3. Work Opportunities

International students in Australia have the opportunity to work part-time while studying. This provides an excellent opportunity to earn money and gain work experience while studying. Additionally, after graduation, students can apply for a post-study work visa, which allows them to work in Australia for up to three years, depending on their qualifications.

4. Beautiful Landscape

Australia is known for its beautiful landscape, with stunning beaches, mountains, and wildlife. Studying in Australia provides an opportunity to explore the country's natural beauty and experience its unique flora and fauna.

5. Safe and Welcoming Environment

Australia is known for its safe and welcoming environment, making it an ideal place for international students to study. The country has strict laws and regulations that ensure the safety of its citizens and visitors. Additionally, Australian universities have support services specifically designed for international students, including language support, career advice, and accommodation assistance.

6. High Standard of Living

Australia has a high standard of living, with excellent healthcare, public transportation, and infrastructure. The country's high standard of living ensures that students have access to all the necessary amenities and services to make their stay in Australia comfortable and enjoyable.

In conclusion, studying in Australia provides a unique opportunity to experience a high-quality education system, diverse culture, beautiful landscape, work opportunities, safe and welcoming environment, and high standard of living. With all these benefits, it's no wonder that Australia has become one of the top destinations for international students.

E. New Zealand

New Zealand is a small island country located in the southwestern Pacific Ocean. It is known for its stunning natural beauty, friendly people, and high-quality education system. Studying in New Zealand can be an excellent opportunity for students looking to enhance their education and gain valuable life experiences. In this article, we will explore the reasons why studying in New Zealand can be an excellent choice for international students.

1. High-Quality Education System: New Zealand has an excellent education system that is internationally recognized for its high-quality standards. The country's universities and institutions are known for their research and innovation, and they offer a wide range of programs and degrees in various fields of study.

2. Affordable Education: Studying in New Zealand can be relatively affordable compared to other popular study destinations such as the United States or the United Kingdom. The cost of living in New Zealand is also lower than in many other developed countries, making it a more cost-effective study option.

3. Safe and Friendly Environment: New Zealand is known for its welcoming and friendly people, making it a safe and comfortable environment for international students. The country has a low crime rate, and its cities are generally considered safe and easy to navigate.

4. Stunning Natural Beauty:

New Zealand is known for its breathtaking landscapes, including mountains, beaches, forests, and lakes. The country's natural beauty provides an excellent opportunity for students to explore and engage in outdoor activities, such as hiking, skiing, and surfing.

5. Multicultural Society:

New Zealand is a multicultural society that celebrates diversity and inclusivity. International students can expect to feel welcomed and accepted in the country, and they can learn from a wide range of cultural perspectives.

6. Work Opportunities:

International students in New Zealand are allowed to work part-time while studying, providing an excellent opportunity to gain work experience and supplement their income.

7. Post-Study Work Visa:

After completing their studies, international students may be eligible for a post-study work visa, allowing them to gain work experience in New Zealand for up to three years.In conclusion, studying in New Zealand offers international students an opportunity to experience high-quality education, a welcoming and diverse culture, stunning natural beauty, and valuable work experience. The country's safe and friendly environment, affordable education, and post-study work visa options make it an excellent study destination for students from around the world.

F.Europe

Europe is a diverse and culturally rich continent that offers an excellent opportunity for international students to enhance their education and gain valuable life experiences. Studying in Europe can be an excellent choice for students looking to broaden their horizons, immerse themselves in different cultures, and gain a world-class education. In this article, we will explore the reasons why studying in Europe can be an excellent option for international students.

1. World-Class Education System:

Europe is home to some of the world's oldest and most prestigious universities, including the University of Oxford, the University of Cambridge, and the University of Paris. European universities are renowned for their high-quality education, innovative research, and diverse range of

2. Academic programs.

Diverse Cultures and Languages: Europe is a continent with a rich cultural heritage and a diverse range of languages. Studying in Europe can provide an opportunity for students to immerse themselves in different cultures, learn new languages, and gain a deeper understanding of the world.

3. Travel Opportunities:

Europe is a relatively small continent, making it easy and affordable to travel between different countries. Studying in Europe provides an excellent opportunity to explore different cultures and countries, and experience new foods, music, and art.

4. Career Opportunities:

Europe is home to many global companies and international organizations, making it an excellent destination for students looking to gain valuable work experience and build their professional network.

5. Multilingual Environment:

Europe is a multilingual continent, and many universities offer courses in different languages, making it an excellent opportunity for students to learn and practice new languages.

6. Affordable Education:

Many universities in Europe offer affordable or free tuition, making it an attractive study destination for students looking to reduce their educational expenses.

7. Vibrant Student Life:

European universities are known for their vibrant student life, with a range of social, cultural, and sporting activities. This provides an excellent opportunity for international students to meet new people, make friends, and integrate into the local community.

In conclusion, studying in Europe offers international students an opportunity to experience a world-class education system, immerse themselves in different cultures, and gain valuable life experiences. Europe's diverse cultures and languages, travel opportunities, career prospects, multilingual environment, affordable education, and vibrant student life make it an attractive study destination for students from around the world.

G. Asia

Asia is a vast and diverse continent, home to some of the world's fastest-growing economies and culturally rich countries. Studying in Asia can be an excellent choice for students looking to enhance their education, immerse themselves in different cultures, and gain valuable life experiences. In this article, we will explore the reasons why studying in Asia can be an excellent option for international students.

1. High-Quality Education System:

Asia is home to some of the world's leading universities, such as the National University of Singapore, the University of Tokyo, and Peking University. Asian universities are known for their high-quality education, innovative research, and diverse range of academic programs.

2. Diverse Cultures and Languages:

Asia is a continent with a rich cultural heritage and a diverse range of languages. Studying in Asia can provide an opportunity for students to immerse themselves in different cultures, learn new languages, and gain a deeper understanding of the world.

3. Growing Economies:

Asia is home to some of the world's fastest-growing economies, such as China, India, and Singapore. Studying in Asia provides an excellent opportunity for students to gain a first-hand understanding of these emerging markets and build their professional network.

4. Travel Opportunities:

Asia is a vast continent, making it easy and affordable to travel between different countries. Studying in Asia provides an excellent opportunity to explore different cultures and countries, and experience new foods, music, and art.

5. Multilingual Environment:

Asia is a multilingual continent, and many universities offer courses in different languages, making it an excellent opportunity for students to learn and practice new languages.

6. Affordable Education:

Many universities in Asia offer affordable tuition fees, making it an attractive study destination for students looking to reduce their educational expenses.

7. Technological Advancements:

Asia is known for its technological advancements, particularly in the areas of artificial intelligence, robotics, and biotechnology. Studying in Asia provides an opportunity for students to gain valuable insights into these cutting-edge technologies and their applications in various industries. In conclusion, studying in Asia offers international students an opportunity to experience a high-quality education system, immerse themselves in different cultures, and gain valuable life experiences.

Asia's diverse cultures and languages, growing economies, travel opportunities, multilingual environment, affordable education, and technological advancements make it an attractive study destination for students from around the world.

Preparing for Study Abroad After 12th

A. Identifying your goals

Studying abroad can be a life-changing experience, providing students with the opportunity to broaden their horizons, gain new perspectives, and develop valuable skills. However, before embarking on this journey, it is essential to identify your goals and objectives to make the most of your study abroad experience. In this article, we will explore how to identify your goals while preparing for study abroad after the 12th. Academic Goals: One of the most common reasons students choose to study abroad is to pursue their academic interests. Before applying to study abroad

1. Academic Goals:

One of the most common reasons students choose to study abroad is to pursue their academic interests. Before applying for study abroad programs, it is essential to identify your academic goals, such as the specific courses or majors you wish to pursue, and the academic requirements you need to meet.

2. Career Goals:

Studying abroad can provide students with valuable work experience and opportunities to build their professional network. Identifying your career goals, such as the industries you are interested in or the job roles you want to pursue, can help you choose the right study abroad program and make the most of your experience.

3. Cultural Goals:

Studying abroad provides an opportunity to immerse yourself in different cultures, learn new languages, and gain a deeper understanding of the world.

Identifying your cultural goals, such as the countries or cultures you want to explore, can help you choose the right study abroad program and make the most of your experience.

4. Personal Goals:

Studying abroad can be a transformative experience, providing students with opportunities for personal growth and development. Identifying your personal goals, such as developing independence, building resilience, or improving language skills, can help you choose the right study abroad program and make the most of your experience.

5. Financial Goals:

Studying abroad can be an expensive endeavor, and it is essential to identify your financial goals and plan accordingly. This includes setting a budget, applying for scholarships or financial aid, and researching cost-effective study abroad programs.

In conclusion, identifying your goals is crucial when preparing for study abroad after the 12th. By identifying your academic, career, cultural, personal, and financial goals, you can choose the right study abroad program and make the most of your experience. Studying abroad can provide an excellent opportunity to broaden your horizons, gain valuable skills, and develop new perspectives, making it a life-changing experience for many students. In conclusion, identifying your goals is crucial when preparing for study abroad after the 12th.

B. Choosing the right program and university

Choosing the right study abroad program and university is crucial when preparing for study abroad after the 12th. It can have a significant impact on your study abroad experience and can determine the success of your academic and personal goals. In this article, we will explore how to choose the right program and university when preparing to study abroad after the 12th.

1. **Research Programs and Universities:**

Start by researching different study abroad programs and universities that offer the courses and majors you are interested in. Consider factors such as location, academic reputation, course offerings, cost, and the availability of scholarships or financial aid.

2. **Consider Your Academic and Career Goals:**

Choose a study abroad program and university that aligns with your academic and career goals. Consider the academic requirements, internships or work experience opportunities, and the reputation of the university in your field of study.

3. **Evaluate Program Structure:**

Evaluate the structure of the study abroad program and university, including the course format, academic workload, and availability of academic resources such as libraries and research facilities.

4. **Consider the Student's Life:**

Studying abroad is not just about academics; it's also an opportunity to immerse yourself in a new culture and experience student life. Consider factors such as student organizations, extracurricular activities, housing options, and the availability of support services such as counseling and health services.

5. **Language Requirements:**

If you are interested in studying in a non-English speaking country, consider the language requirements of the study abroad program and university.

6. Speak to Alumni and Advisors:
Speak to alumni of the study abroad program and university and seek advice from study abroad advisors to gain valuable insights into the program structure, academic workload, and student life.

In conclusion, choosing the right study abroad program and university is crucial when preparing for study abroad after the 12th. Consider factors such as academic and career goals, program structure, student life, and language requirements, and seek advice from alumni and advisors. By taking the time to research and evaluate study abroad programs and universities, you can ensure that you have a successful and rewarding study abroad experience.

C. Conducting research on the destination country

When preparing for study abroad after the 12th, conducting research on the destination country is essential to have a successful and enjoyable experience. By researching the country's culture, history, customs, and lifestyle, you can prepare for the academic and social aspects of studying abroad. In this article, we will explore how to conduct research on the destination country when preparing to study abroad after the 12th.

1. **Start with General Information:**

Begin by researching general information about the country, such as its geography, climate, population, language, and currency. This will give you a basic understanding of the country and its people.

2. **Study the Culture and Customs:**

Study the country's culture, customs, and social norms. This includes understanding the values, traditions, and etiquette of the country, as well as the local cuisine, music, and art. This will help you to understand and respect the local culture and avoid any cultural misunderstandings.

3. **Learn about the Education System:**

Learn about the country's education system, including the structure of the university system, academic standards, and grading system. This will help you to understand the academic expectations and requirements of your study abroad program.

4. **Explore Local Attractions and Activities:**

Research the local attractions and activities in the destination country, such as museums, historical sites, festivals, and outdoor activities. This will give you a sense of what the country has to offer beyond academics and can help you to plan your leisure time.

5. Stay Informed about Current Events:

Stay informed about current events in the destination country by following local news sources, social media, and other media outlets. This will help you to understand the political and social climate of the country and prepare for any potential challenges or disruptions.

6. Connect with Other Students:

Connect with other students who have studied abroad in the destination country, either through social media or your study abroad program. They can provide valuable insights and advice on the country's culture, lifestyle, and academic requirements.

In conclusion, conducting research on the destination country is crucial when preparing for study abroad after the 12th. By researching the country's culture, history, customs, and lifestyle, you can prepare for the academic and social aspects of studying abroad. Consider starting with general information, studying the culture and customs, learning about the education system, exploring local attractions and activities, staying informed about current events, and connecting with other students. By taking the time to research the destination country, you can have a successful and enjoyable study abroad experience.

D. Obtaining necessary travel documents

Obtaining necessary travel documents is an essential part of preparing for study abroad after the 12th. The process of obtaining travel documents can be time-consuming and complex, but it is essential to ensure a smooth and successful study abroad experience. In this article, we will explore the steps to obtain necessary travel documents when preparing for study abroad after the 12th.

1. Check Passport Requirements:

Ensure that you have a valid passport with an expiration date that is at least six months after your planned return date. If you don't have a passport, apply for one as soon as possible.

2. Apply for a Visa:

Depending on the destination country and the length of your stay, you may need to apply for a student visa. Check with the embassy or consulate of the destination country to determine if a visa is required and how to apply.

3. Obtain Health and Travel Insurance:

Some study abroad programs require students to have health and travel insurance. Even if it is not required, it is highly recommended to have insurance coverage in case of any unforeseen medical or travel-related issues.

4. Research COVID-19 Requirements:

Due to the COVID-19 pandemic, many countries have implemented travel restrictions and health requirements. Check the destination country's COVID-19 guidelines, including quarantine requirements and any necessary vaccinations.

5. Obtain Required Vaccinations:

Some countries require specific vaccinations to enter the country.

Check with the embassy or consulate of the destination country to determine what vaccinations are required and obtain them before traveling.

6. Pack Important Documents:
Make sure to pack all necessary documents, such as your passport, visa, health insurance card, and any other necessary travel documents. Keep them in a secure location and easily accessible in case of emergency.

In conclusion, obtaining the necessary travel documents is crucial when preparing for study abroad after the 12th. It is essential to check passport requirements, apply for a visa, obtain health and travel insurance, research COVID-19 requirements, obtain required vaccinations, and pack important documents. By taking the necessary steps to obtain travel documents, you can ensure a smooth and successful study abroad experience.

E. Preparing financially for study abroad

Preparing financially for study abroad after the 12th is a critical step in ensuring a successful and stress-free experience. Studying abroad can be costly, and it is important to plan and budget accordingly to avoid any financial difficulties during your program. In this article, we will explore some essential tips to prepare financially for study abroad after the 12th.

1. Research Costs:

Research the cost of living, tuition fees, accommodation, and travel expenses in the destination country. This will give you a better understanding of how much you will need to budget for the program.

2. Explore Scholarship Opportunities:

Many study abroad programs offer scholarships or financial aid. Research and apply for scholarships that fit your academic achievements, interests, and financial needs.

3. Consider Part-Time Work:

If you are allowed to work part-time while studying abroad, consider taking up a part-time job to supplement your income. However, make sure to check the work visa requirements and restrictions in the destination country before planning to work.

4. Create a Budget:

Create a realistic budget that includes all your expenses, such as tuition fees, accommodation, food, travel expenses, and other expenses. Stick to the budget and avoid overspending.

5. Save Money:

Start saving money well in advance of your study abroad program. Look for ways to cut expenses, such as eating out less frequently or reducing unnecessary purchases. Consider working a part-time job before your program to save money.

6. Consult with a Financial Advisor:

Consider consulting with a financial advisor to discuss your financial situation and to create a plan for financing your study abroad program.

5. Use Student Discounts:

Many businesses offer student discounts on various goods and services. Make sure to take advantage of these discounts to save money.

In conclusion, preparing financially for study abroad after 12th requires careful planning and budgeting. Research the costs of the program, explore scholarship opportunities, consider part-time work, create a budget, save money, consult with a financial advisor, and use student discounts. By taking the necessary steps to prepare financially, you can avoid any financial difficulties during your study abroad program and have a successful experience

F. Getting immunizations and health insurance

Getting immunizations and health insurance is an essential part of preparing for study abroad after 12th. When studying abroad, you may be exposed to different health risks, and it is important to take the necessary steps to protect yourself. In this article, we will explore the importance of getting immunizations and health insurance when preparing for study abroad after 12th.

Getting Immunizations

Immunizations are important to protect against diseases that may not be prevalent in your home country. Many countries have specific immunization requirements for entry, so it is important to check with the embassy or consulate of the destination country to determine which immunizations are required.

In addition to mandatory immunizations, it is also important to consider other recommended immunizations based on the destination country and the type of program. For example, if you are studying in a tropical region, you may need to get immunized against malaria, yellow fever, or other mosquito-borne illnesses. You can consult with your doctor or a travel health clinic to determine which additional immunizations are recommended for your destination.

Getting Health Insurance

Having health insurance is essential when studying abroad as it can help cover the costs of medical treatment, emergency care, and evacuation. Many study abroad programs require students to have health insurance, but even if it is not required, it is highly recommended to have coverage.

Before selecting a health insurance plan, research the coverage options available and make sure it covers medical care in the destination country. Make sure to check the policy details, including deductibles, copays, and maximum coverage limits.

It is also important to carry a copy of your health insurance card with you at all times in case of emergency.

Other Considerations

In addition to getting immunizations and health insurance, there are other important considerations to keep in mind when preparing for study abroad after the 12th. These include:

- **Researching the quality of healthcare in the destination country**
- **Bringing necessary medications with you**
- **Identifying emergency medical facilities in the area**
- **Knowing how to access medical care in case of emergency**

In conclusion, getting immunizations and health insurance is crucial when preparing for study abroad after the 12th. It is important to research which immunizations are required and recommended for your destination and to choose a health insurance plan that provides adequate coverage. By taking the necessary steps to protect your health, you can have a safe and successful study abroad experience.

Financing Your Study Abroad Experience

A. Budgeting for study abroad

Studying abroad can be an exciting and life-changing experience, but it can also be expensive. Budgeting for study abroad is an essential part of the preparation process to ensure that you can afford the program fees, travel costs, accommodation, and living expenses in the destination country. In this article, we will explore the importance of budgeting for study abroad and provide some tips to help you manage your finances. Why is budgeting important for studying abroad?

Budgeting is essential for study abroad for several reasons:

1. To manage costs:

Studying abroad can be expensive, and without a budget, it is easy to overspend. Budgeting helps you manage your finances and ensures that you do not run out of money before the end of the program.

2..To plan ahead:

Knowing how much you can afford to spend before you leave will allow you to plan your expenses and avoid unexpected financial issues.

3. **To maximize your experience:**

Budgeting helps you plan ahead and allocate funds for the activities and experiences that are most important to you while studying abroad.

Tips for budgeting for study abroad:

1. Research the costs:

Before you start budgeting, research the costs of the program, accommodation, and living expenses in the destination country. This will help you get an accurate idea of how much you will need to spend.

2. Create a budget:

Once you have an idea of the costs, create a budget that includes your income, expenses, and savings. Consider all costs, including travel, accommodation, food, and entertainment.

3. Look for scholarships and financial aid:

Many programs offer scholarships and financial aid to help students cover the costs of studying abroad. Research these options and apply for any that you are eligible for.

4. Save money before you go:

If possible, start saving money for your study abroad program before you go. This will help you avoid taking on too much debt and allow you to have a more comfortable experience.

5. Monitor your expenses:

Once you are abroad, monitor your expenses closely and adjust your budget as needed. Use a mobile app or spreadsheet to track your spending and ensure that you are staying within your budget.

6. Find ways to save money:

Look for ways to save money while abroad, such as cooking your meals instead of eating out, using public transportation instead of taxis, and taking advantage of free activities and events.

In conclusion, budgeting for study abroad is essential to ensure that you can afford the program fees, travel costs, accommodation, and living expenses in the destination country.

By researching the costs, creating a budget, looking for scholarships and financial aid, saving money before you go, monitoring your expenses, and finding ways to save money, you can manage your finances and have a successful study abroad experience.

B. Identifying sources of funding

Studying abroad can be an enriching and life-changing experience, but it can also be expensive. Many students may feel discouraged by the cost of studying abroad and wonder how they will afford it. Fortunately, there are various sources of funding available to help finance a study abroad program. In this article, we will explore the different sources of funding for studying abroad

1. Scholarships and grants:

Scholarships and grants are often available to students studying abroad. These can be offered by the university, government, non-profit organizations, or private foundations. Scholarships and grants may cover some or all of the program costs, including tuition fees, accommodation, and travel expenses. To apply for these scholarships and grants, students will usually need to submit an application and meet certain eligibility criteria, such as academic achievement or financial need.

2. Student loans:

Many banks and financial institutions offer student loans specifically for studying abroad. These loans can help students cover the cost of tuition fees, travel, and living expenses. However, students should be cautious when taking out a loan and carefully consider the repayment terms, interest rates, and fees before committing to borrowing.

3. Work-study programs:

Some universities offer work-study programs for students studying abroad. These programs allow students to work part-time while studying, which can help cover some of the costs of their program. Work-study programs may include jobs such as teaching assistants, research assistants, or administrative assistants.

4. Personal savings:

Students can use their personal savings to fund their study abroad program. This may include money saved from part-time jobs or other sources of income. Students should start saving early and make a budget to ensure they have enough money to cover their program costs.

5. Crowdfunding:

Crowdfunding platforms such as GoFundMe or Kickstarter can be used to raise funds for a study abroad program. Students can create a campaign explaining their study abroad goals and why they need funding. Friends, family, and other supporters can then donate to the campaign.

6. Employer-sponsored programs:

Some employers offer study abroad programs for their employees or provide financial assistance for employees who want to study abroad. Students should check with their employers to see if such programs are available.

In conclusion, studying abroad can be an expensive endeavor, but there are various sources of funding available to help finance a study abroad program. Scholarships and grants, student loans, work-study programs, personal savings, crowdfunding, and employer-sponsored programs are all possible sources of funding. Students should research and apply for all available funding opportunities and make a budget to ensure they can cover their program costs.

C. Applying for scholarships and grants

Studying abroad can be an incredible experience, but it can also be expensive. Luckily, there are scholarships and grants available to help students fund their study abroad programs. In this article, we will explore the steps involved in applying for scholarships and grants for study abroad.

Step 1: Research available scholarships and grants

The first step is to research the scholarships and grants that are available for study abroad programs. This can be done by searching online, visiting your university's study abroad office, and speaking with your academic advisor. Make a list of the scholarships and grants that you are eligible for, and be sure to note their application deadlines and requirements.

Step 2: Meet the eligibility criteria

Each scholarship or grant will have its own eligibility criteria. These may include academic performance, financial need, language proficiency, or participation in certain extracurricular activities. Be sure to carefully review the eligibility requirements for each scholarship or grant that you are interested in and make sure that you meet them.

Step 3: Prepare your application materials

The application requirements for scholarships and grants will vary, but common materials include transcripts, essays, letters of recommendation, and proof of financial need. Make sure to carefully review the application requirements and prepare all necessary materials ahead of time. It is important to note that some scholarships and grants require you to submit your application in the language of the country where you will be studying, so you may need to have your application materials translated.

Step 4: Submit your application

Once you have prepared your application materials, it is time to submit your application. Be sure to carefully follow the application instructions and submit your application by the deadline. If you are mailing your application, be sure to send it with enough time for it to arrive before the deadline.

Step 5: Follow up

After you have submitted your application, it is important to follow up with the scholarship or grant provider. Make sure to check your email and mailbox regularly for any updates or requests for additional information. If you receive an award, be sure to thank the scholarship or grant provider and follow any instructions they provide for accepting the award.

in conclusion, applying for scholarships and grants for study abroad can be a time-consuming process, but it is worth the effort. By researching available scholarships and grants, meeting eligibility criteria, preparing your application materials, submitting your application on time, and following up, you can increase your chances of receiving funding for your study abroad program. Remember to start early, be organized, and put forth your best effort when applying for scholarships and grants.

D. Applying for loans

Studying abroad can be an incredible experience, but it can also be expensive. If you are unable to cover the costs of your study abroad program with scholarships, grants, or personal savings, you may need to consider taking out a loan. In this article, we will explore the steps involved in applying for loans to study abroad.

Step 1: Research available loan options
The first step is to research the loan options that are available for study abroad programs. This can be done by searching online, visiting your bank or credit union, and speaking with your university's financial aid office. Be sure to note the interest rates, repayment terms, and any fees associated with each loan option.

Step 2: Determine how much you need to borrow
Before applying for a loan, you need to determine how much money you need to borrow. This includes tuition and fees, housing, meals, transportation, and any other expenses associated with your study abroad program. Be sure to factor in the exchange rate and any additional expenses related to living in a foreign country.

Step3: Apply for the loan
Once you have determined how much money you need to borrow, it is time to apply for the loan. This typically involves submitting an application, providing documentation of your income and credit history, and undergoing a credit check. If you are under the age of 18, you may need a cosigner to be approved for the loan.

Step 4: Review and sign the loan agreement
If your loan application is approved, you will receive a loan agreement that outlines the terms and conditions of the loan.

Be sure to review the agreement carefully, paying special attention to the interest rate, repayment terms, and any fees. If you have any questions, do not hesitate to ask the lender for clarification.

Step 5: Receive the loan funds

After you have signed the loan agreement, the loan funds will be disbursed to you or directly to the university. Be sure to use the funds only for the purposes specified in the loan agreement.

Step 6: Repay the loan

Once you have completed your study abroad program, you will need to begin repaying the loan. Be sure to make your payments on time and in full to avoid late fees and damage to your credit score. If you experience financial hardship, contact your lender to explore options for deferment or forbearance.

In conclusion, taking out a loan to study abroad can be a viable option if you are unable to cover the costs of your program through other means. However, it is important to carefully research loan options, determine how much you need to borrow, apply for the loan, review and sign the loan agreement, receive the loan funds, and repay the loan on time. By following these steps, you can make an informed decision about whether a loan is the right option for funding your study abroad program.

Cultural Differences and Adjusting to Life Abroad

A. Understanding cultural differences

One of the most exciting aspects of studying abroad is the opportunity to immerse yourself in a different culture. However, it's important to understand that cultural differences can also create challenges and require adjustment. In this article, we will explore how to understand and navigate cultural differences while studying abroad.

1. Do your research

Before you go, take the time to research the culture of your destination country. Learn about their history, customs, values, and traditions. This will give you a foundation for understanding and appreciating their way of life

2. Observe and listen

Once you arrive, be observant and listen to the locals. Pay attention to their body language, communication styles, and social norms. This will help you understand their perspective and avoid misunderstandings.

3. Be open-minded

It's important to approach cultural differences with an open mind. Don't assume that your way of doing things is the only way, and be willing to try new things. This will help you adapt to the culture and build relationships with locals.

4. Be respectful

Respect is a universal value, and it's especially important when it comes to cultural differences. Be respectful of local customs and traditions, even if they are different from your own. This includes things like dress codes, greetings, and dining etiquette.

5. Build relationships

One of the best ways to understand a culture is to build relationships with locals. Attend social events, join clubs and organizations, and participate in cultural activities. This will give you a deeper understanding of their way of life and help you feel more connected to the community.

6. Seek support

Adjusting to a new culture can be challenging, so don't hesitate to seek support if you need it. This can include talking to other students in your program, seeking advice from local resources, or connecting with a mentor or advisor.

7. Reflect on your own culture

Finally, take the time to reflect on your own culture and how it shapes your perspective. This will help you understand and appreciate the differences in the culture of your destination country.

In conclusion, understanding cultural differences is an important aspect of studying abroad. By doing your research, observing and listening, being open-minded and respectful, building relationships, seeking support, and reflecting on your own culture, you can navigate cultural differences and make the most of your study abroad experience.

B. Navigating the language barrier

Navigating the language barrier can be one of the biggest challenges for students studying abroad. Here are some tips to help you overcome this hurdle and make the most of your study abroad experience:

1. Learn the language before you go

The best way to navigate the language barrier is to learn the language before you go. Take a language course at your home institution or enroll in a language school in the destination country. This will help you communicate more effectively and immerse yourself in the culture.

2. Practice with locals

Once you arrive, practice speaking the language with the locals. Don't be afraid to make mistakes - it's a natural part of the learning process. Practice in everyday situations like ordering food or asking for directions, and seek feedback from native speakers.

3. Use language-learning apps

There are many language-learning apps available that can help you practice and improve your language skills. Some popular options include Duolingo, Rosetta Stone, and Babbel. These apps can be a convenient and effective way to practice on the go.

4. Watch TV shows and movies in the local language

Watching TV shows and movies in the local language can help you improve your listening and comprehension skills. This can also be a fun way to immerse yourself in the local culture and learn more about the country.

5. Use translation apps and dictionaries

If you're struggling to communicate with locals, consider using translation apps or dictionaries.

These tools can be a helpful backup when you don't know a specific word or phrase.

6. Seek language exchange opportunities

Language exchange programs can be a great way to practice your language skills and make new friends. Look for language exchange opportunities through local schools, community centers, or online forums.

7. Stay positive

Finally, remember to stay positive and have fun! Navigating the language barrier can be challenging, but it's also a great opportunity to learn and grow. Embrace the experience and don't be afraid to make mistakes.

In conclusion, navigating the language barrier can be a challenge, but with the right mindset and tools, it's possible to overcome. By learning the language before you go, practicing with locals, using language-learning apps and tools, seeking language exchange opportunities, and staying positive, you can make the most of your study abroad experience and improve your language skills.

C.Developing cross-cultural communication skills

Developing cross-cultural communication skills is an important aspect of studying abroad. Here are some tips to help you navigate cultural differences and communicate effectively with people from diverse backgrounds:

1. Be open-minded and respectful

The first step in developing cross-cultural communication skills is to approach every interaction with an open mind and respect for other cultures. Be willing to learn and adapt to new customs and ways of thinking.

2. Learn about the local culture

Take the time to learn about the local culture before you go. This can help you avoid cultural faux pas and understand the values and customs of the people you will be interacting with.

3. Communicate clearly

When communicating with people from different cultures, it's important to speak clearly and avoid idioms or expressions that may not translate well. Use simple, straightforward language and be patient if there are communication barriers.

4. Pay attention to nonverbal cues

In many cultures, nonverbal cues like eye contact, hand gestures, and body language can be just as important as verbal communication. Pay attention to these cues and try to interpret them in the context of the culture you are in.

5. Practice active listening

Active listening is a key component of effective cross-cultural communication. Listen carefully to what others are saying and ask clarifying questions if necessary. Show that you are engaged and interested in what they have to say.

6. **Embrace differences**

Instead of focusing on differences as obstacles, try to embrace them as opportunities to learn and grow. Celebrate diversity and seek out new perspectives and experiences.

7. **Reflect on your own cultural biases**

Finally, take the time to reflect on your own cultural biases and assumptions. Be aware of how your own culture may influence your communication style and be willing to adapt as needed.

In conclusion, developing cross-cultural communication skills is essential for a successful study abroad experience. By approaching every interaction with an open mind and respect, learning about the local culture, communicating clearly, paying attention to nonverbal cues, practicing active listening, embracing differences, and reflecting on your own cultural biases, you can navigate cultural differences and communicate effectively with people from diverse backgrounds.

D. Adapting to local customs and norms

Studying abroad provides a unique opportunity to experience different cultures and customs. Adapting to local customs and norms is an important part of immersing oneself in a new culture and making the most of the study abroad experience. Here are some tips for adapting to local customs and norms while studying abroad

1. Observe and learn

Take the time to observe and learn about the local customs and norms. This can be done by reading about the local culture before arriving, watching and learning from locals, and asking questions when in doubt. It is important to respect local customs and be open to new experiences.

2. Show respect

It is important to show respect to the local culture by adhering to local customs and norms. This can include dressing appropriately, showing respect to elders, and being mindful of local customs during religious ceremonies and other events.

3. Be flexible

Be open and flexible to change. Local customs may differ from what you are accustomed to, and it is important to be flexible and adaptable to new ways of doing things. Be prepared to adjust your expectations and embrace new experiences.

4. Make an effort to communicate

Communication is key in adapting to local customs and norms. Make an effort to communicate with locals, learn the local language or at least some key phrases, and practice active listening.

5. Build relationships

Building relationships with locals is a great way to learn more about the local customs and norms. Join local clubs or organizations, volunteer, and attend community events to connect with locals.

6. **Don't judge**

Avoid being judgmental about local customs and norms. Just because something may be different from what you are accustomed to does not make it wrong. Be open to learning and understanding different perspectives.

7. **Stay safe**

While it is important to adapt to local customs and norms, it is also important to stay safe. Be aware of any safety concerns in the local area and follow local laws and regulations.

In conclusion, adapting to local customs and norms is an important part of the study abroad experience. By observing and learning, showing respect, being flexible, communicating, building relationships, avoiding judgment, and staying safe, you can embrace new experiences and fully immerse yourself in the local culture.

E. Coping with homesickness

Studying abroad is an exciting opportunity to experience new cultures, make new friends, and learn new things. However, it can also be challenging to be away from home for an extended period of time. Feeling homesick is a common experience for students studying abroad, but there are ways to cope with these feelings and make the most of the study abroad experience.

1. Stay connected with family and friends back home

One of the most important things you can do to cope with homesickness is to stay connected with family and friends back home. Thanks to technology, it's easier than ever to keep in touch through video calls, messaging, and social media. Set a regular time to talk with your loved ones, but also try to immerse yourself in the local culture and make new friends.

2. Embrace the new culture

One of the best ways to overcome homesickness is to immerse yourself in the local culture. Try new foods, attend local events, and participate in cultural activities. This can help you feel more connected to your new surroundings and make new friends.

3. Stay busy

Keeping yourself busy can also help with homesickness. Take advantage of your study abroad program's activities and excursions, join a local club or organization, or explore your new city. Filling your time with new experiences can help you focus on the present and enjoy your study abroad experience.

4. Practice self-care

Homesickness can be stressful, so it's important to take care of yourself. Get enough sleep, eat healthy meals, exercise regularly, and take time for yourself.

Engage in activities that you enjoy and that help you relax, like reading, listening to music, or practicing yoga.

5. Talk to someone

If you are struggling with homesickness, don't hesitate to talk to someone about your feelings. This could be a friend, a family member, a program advisor, or a mental health professional. It's normal to feel homesick, but it's also important to take care of your mental health and seek support if you need it.

In conclusion, feeling homesick is a common experience when studying abroad, but there are ways to cope with these feelings and make the most of the study abroad experience. Staying connected with loved ones, embracing the new culture, staying busy, practicing self-care, and talking to someone are all effective ways to manage homesickness and enjoy your time abroad.

Finding Housing and Settling In

A. Finding suitable accommodation

Studying abroad is an exciting opportunity to experience a new culture, learn a new language, and gain a valuable education. However, one of the most crucial aspects of studying abroad is finding suitable accommodation. Finding a comfortable and safe place to stay can help you concentrate on your studies and enjoy your experience without worrying about where you will sleep at night. In this article, we will provide some tips to help you find suitable accommodation for studying abroad.

1. Research the location

Before you start looking for accommodation, it is essential to research the location where you will be studying. Check the cost of living, the safety of the area, the public transportation system, and the availability of accommodation. This research will give you an idea of what to expect and help you budget accordingly.

2. Start your search early

Start your search for accommodation as soon as you can. It may take longer than you expect to find suitable accommodation, especially during peak season. Starting your search early will give you enough time to find a suitable place that meets your requirements and budget.

3. Check the University's accommodation options

Many universities offer accommodation options to their international students. These options include on-campus dormitories, apartments, and homestays. Check the university's website for more information on these options and how to apply.

On-campus accommodation is a popular choice for international students as it is convenient, safe, and provides an opportunity to meet other students.

4. Look for student housing options

There are many student housing options available in most countries, and they cater to students' needs. These housing options are usually affordable, and you get to live with other students, which is an excellent opportunity to make friends and explore the local culture. You can find student housing options on websites such as Student.com, Uniplaces, and HousingAnywhere.

5. Consider homestays

Homestays are a great way to immerse yourself in the local culture and practice the language. A homestay involves living with a host family in their home, and they provide you with a room and meals. Homestays are often less expensive than other accommodation options, and you get to experience the local culture firsthand. You can find homestays on websites such as Homestay.com and Homestayin.com.

6. Use rental websites

Rental websites such as Airbnb, Booking.com, and Agoda are excellent options for finding short-term accommodation. These websites offer a range of options, from budget-friendly to luxurious. When using these websites, ensure that you read the reviews and check the location to ensure that it is safe and convenient.

7. Consider your budget

When looking for accommodation, it is essential to consider your budget. Your accommodation expenses should not exceed 30% of your total budget.

Consider the cost of living in the location and factor in other expenses such as food, transportation, and entertainment. It is also essential to consider the deposit, rent, and other fees associated with the accommodation.

In conclusion, finding suitable accommodation for studying abroad requires some research and planning. Start your search early, consider your budget, and look for options such as on-campus accommodation, student housing, homestays, and rental websites. By following these tips, you can find a comfortable and safe place to stay and enjoy your study abroad experience to the fullest

B. Getting familiar with the local area

Studying abroad can be a thrilling experience, but it can also be challenging to adjust to a new environment. One of the most important things you can do to make your study abroad program more comfortable is to get familiar with the local area. By exploring your new surroundings, you can better adapt to your new surroundings and feel more at home. Here are some tips on how to get familiar with the local area during your study abroad program

1. Take a walking tour

One of the best ways to explore a new place is by taking a walking tour. Many cities offer free walking tours, and they are a great way to learn about the history, culture, and landmarks of the area. Walking tours are also a great way to meet new people and make friends.

2. Use public transportation

Using public transportation is an excellent way to get around and explore your new surroundings. It is also a great way to familiarize yourself with the local transportation system. Take a bus or a train and see where it takes you. You can also download local transportation apps, such as Moovit, Citymapper, or Google Maps, to help you navigate the local transportation system.

3. Join a local club or organization

Joining a local club or organization is a great way to meet new people and get involved in the local community. Look for clubs or organizations that interest you, such as sports teams, language exchange clubs, or cultural groups. Joining a local club or organization can help you feel more connected to your new environment and make your study abroad experience more enjoyable

4.Visit local markets

Visiting local markets is an excellent way to experience the local culture and try new foods. You can also find unique souvenirs to bring back home. Markets are often held on specific days of the week, so make sure to find out when they are open.

5.Go on weekend trips

Going on weekend trips is an excellent way to explore your new surroundings and see what the surrounding area has to offer. You can plan a trip with your new friends or join a group tour. Weekend trips can also be an excellent opportunity to practice your language skills and learn about the local customs.

6.Attend local events

Attending local events is a great way to experience the local culture and make new friends. Look for events such as festivals, concerts, and sporting events. You can find information about local events on social media, local newspapers, or city websites.

7.Get involved in campus activities

Getting involved in campus activities is an excellent way to meet new people and get involved in your new community. Join a student club or organization or attend campus events. Campus activities can also help you adjust to your new environment and make your study abroad experience more enjoyable.

In conclusion, getting familiar with the local area during your study abroad program can make your experience more enjoyable and help you adjust to your new environment. Take a walking tour, use public transportation, join a local club or organization, visit local markets, go on weekend trips, attend local events, and get involved in campus activities. By following these tips, you can make the most of your study abroad program and create lasting memories.

C. Opening a bank account and getting a mobile phone

When studying abroad, it is important to take care of practical matters such as opening a bank account and getting a mobile phone. These tasks can seem daunting, but they are essential for your everyday life while abroad. Here is a guide on how to open a bank account and get a mobile phone during your study abroad program.

Opening a Bank Account:

1. Research local banks:

Before choosing a bank, research the options available in your destination. Check the banks' websites for information on account types, fees, and services.

2. Determine the documents needed:

Find out what documents you will need to open an account. In most cases, you will need a passport, proof of address, and a student visa. Some banks may also require additional documents, so be sure to check beforehand.

3. Make an appointment:

Call the bank or visit its website to make an appointment. It is essential to schedule an appointment to avoid long wait times.

4. Bring the necessary documents:

Bring all the required documents to your appointment. The bank will review the documents and may require additional information.

5. Deposit funds:

Once your account is open, you will need to deposit funds to start using it. You can transfer money from your home bank account or deposit cash.

Getting a Mobile Phone:
1. **Choose a carrier:**
Research local mobile phone carriers and compare their plans and prices. Check if they offer student discounts.

2. **Determine the documents needed:**
Find out what documents you will need to get a mobile phone. In most cases, you will need a passport and proof of address. Some carriers may require additional documents, so be sure to check beforehand.

3. **Make an appointment:**
Call the carrier or visit its website to make an appointment. It is essential to schedule an appointment to avoid long wait times.

4. **Choose a plan:**
Choose a plan that fits your needs and budget. Most carriers offer prepaid plans that allow you to pay for only the services you use.

5. **Purchase a phone:**
You can either bring your own unlocked phone or purchase a phone from the carrier. Be aware that purchasing a phone may require a contract commitment.

6. **Set up your phone:**
Once you have a phone and a plan, you will need to set up your phone. This involves inserting the SIM card and activating the phone.

In conclusion, opening a bank account and getting a mobile phone are essential tasks when studying abroad. Research local banks and carriers, determine the required documents, make an appointment, choose a plan, and purchase a phone. By following these steps, you can take care of practical matters and enjoy your study abroad program.

D. Setting up utilities and internet service

Setting up utilities and internet service is another essential task when studying abroad. It can be challenging to navigate the process in a foreign country, but it is crucial for your daily life. Here is a guide on how to set up utilities and internet service during your study abroad program.

Setting up Utilities:

1. Research the local utility providers:

Before arriving at your destination, research the local utility providers. Determine which providers offer services in your area, such as gas, water, and electricity.

2. Contact the provider:

Once you arrive, contact the provider to set up your account. You may be able to do this online or over the phone.

3. Provide necessary information:

The provider will require specific information, such as your name, address, and the date you want to start service. They may also require a deposit or proof of address.

4. Schedule an installation appointment:

If necessary, schedule an installation appointment for the provider to set up the service at your residence

Setting up Internet Service:

1. Research the local internet providers:

Research the local internet providers and compare their plans and prices. Determine which provider offers services in your area.

2. Contact the provider:

Contact the provider to set up your account. You may be able to do this online or over the phone.

3. **Provide necessary information:**

The provider will require specific information, such as your name, address, and the date you want to start service. They may also require a deposit or proof of address.

4. **Choose a plan:**

Choose a plan that fits your needs and budget. Most providers offer different speed tiers, so determine how much bandwidth you need.

5. **Schedule an installation appointment:**

Schedule an installation appointment for the provider to set up the internet at your residence.

It is essential to set up utilities and internet service as soon as possible upon arriving at your study abroad destination. These services are crucial for your daily life, and delays can cause unnecessary stress. By researching local providers, providing necessary information, and scheduling installation appointments, you can set up your utilities and internet service quickly and efficiently.

E. Getting involved in extracurricular activities

Getting involved in extracurricular activities is an excellent way to make the most of your study abroad program. Not only can it enhance your cultural experience, but it can also help you develop new skills and make new friends. Here is a guide on how to get involved in extracurricular activities during your study abroad program.

1. Research available activities:
Before you arrive at your destination, research the extracurricular activities available. Check your school's website, social media pages, and flyers around campus.

2. Attend the orientation:
Attend the orientation for international students to learn about the extracurricular activities available. You can also meet other international students who share similar interests.

3. Join a student club:
Join a student club or organization that aligns with your interests. Whether it's a sports team, cultural club, or academic organization, getting involved can help you connect with like-minded students.

4. Attend events and activities:
Attend events and activities on campus or in the community. This could include concerts, festivals, and sporting events.

5. Volunteer:
Consider volunteering at a local organization or community event. Not only can you make a positive impact, but you can also meet locals and practice your language skills.

6. Take advantage of study abroad program excursions:

Many study abroad programs offer excursions to nearby cultural sites, museums, and historical landmarks. Take advantage of these opportunities to learn more about your destination and make new friends.

7. **Explore your surroundings:**

Don't be afraid to explore your surroundings and try new things. Whether it's trying local food, visiting a nearby town, or taking part in outdoor activities, exploring your destination can enhance your experience.

Getting involved in extracurricular activities can help you make the most of your study abroad program. By researching available activities, attending the orientation, joining a student club, attending events, volunteering, taking advantage of excursions, and exploring your surroundings, you can enhance your cultural experience and create unforgettable memories.

Opportunities for Travel and Cultural Immersion

A. Exploring local landmarks and attractions

One of the most exciting things about studying abroad is the opportunity to explore new landmarks and attractions. Whether it's historical monuments, famous museums, or beautiful natural landscapes, there are many things to discover in a new country. Here are some tips on how to explore local landmarks and attractions during your study abroad program:

1. **Research ahead of time:**

Before setting out to explore, do some research on the local landmarks and attractions. Find out the history behind them and their significance to the local culture.

2. **Visit popular tourist destinations:**

Popular tourist destinations are a great way to experience the local culture and history. Make sure to visit the top attractions in the area, such as historical monuments, museums, and landmarks.

3. **Explore off the beaten path:**

While it's important to visit popular tourist destinations, exploring off the beaten path can also lead to some amazing discoveries. Talk to locals and ask for recommendations on hidden gems or lesser-known attractions.

4. **Take a guided tour:**

Taking a guided tour is a great way to learn about the history and culture of the area. Look for guided tours of landmarks and attractions that interest you, or consider a walking tour to get a sense of the local area.

5. Use public transportation:

Using public transportation is a great way to get around and explore the local area. Take a bus or a train to visit attractions that are farther away or in different parts of the city.

6. Attend local festivals and events:

Attending local festivals and events is a great way to experience the local culture and traditions. Look for events related to holidays, music, or food.

7. Take advantage of student discounts:

Many attractions offer student discounts, so make sure to bring your student ID and take advantage of the savings.

8. Take pictures and keep a journal:

Taking pictures and keeping a journal is a great way to remember your experiences and reflect on your study abroad program. Write down your thoughts and feelings, and take plenty of pictures to share with family and friends.

In conclusion, exploring local landmarks and attractions during your study abroad program is an essential part of the experience. Research ahead of time, visit popular tourist destinations, explore off the beaten path, take a guided tour, use public transportation, attend local festivals and events, take advantage of student discounts, and keep a journal. With these tips, you can make the most of your study abroad program and create lasting memories.

B. Joining student clubs and organizations

One of the best ways to fully immerse yourself in a study abroad program is by joining student clubs and organizations. These groups provide an opportunity to meet new people, engage in new activities, and gain a deeper understanding of the local culture. Here are some tips on how to join student clubs and organizations during your study abroad program:

1. Attend the study abroad orientation:

Many study abroad programs offer an orientation session where you can learn about the different clubs and organizations available. Attend this session to get a better understanding of what's available and how to get involved.

2. Look for clubs related to your interests:

Look for clubs and organizations that align with your interests and hobbies. This can be anything from sports teams, language exchange groups, or cultural organizations.

3. Attend the first meeting:

Once you have identified a club or organization that interests you, attend the first meeting to get a feel for the group. This is a great opportunity to meet members and learn more about the group's goals and activities.

4. Volunteer:

Many clubs and organizations organize volunteer events in the local community. This is a great way to give back while also meeting new people and learning about the local culture.

5. Attend social events:

Social events, such as parties or gatherings, are a great way to get to know other members of the club or organization in a more relaxed setting.

Attend these events to build relationships and make new friends.

6. Be open-minded:
Joining a new club or organization can be intimidating, especially in a new country. Be open-minded and willing to try new things. This is a great opportunity to step outside of your comfort zone and learn new skills.

7. Stay committed:
Once you join a club or organization, Make a commitment to stay involved. Attend meetings regularly and participate in events and activities.

In conclusion, joining student clubs and organizations during your study abroad program can enhance your experience and provide a deeper understanding of the local culture. Attend the study abroad orientation, look for clubs related to your interests, attend the first meeting, volunteer, attend social events, be open-minded, and stay committed. With these tips, you can make the most of your study abroad program and build relationships that last a lifetime.

C. Volunteering or interning in the community

Volunteering or interning in the local community during your study abroad program can be a rewarding experience that allows you to give back and make a positive impact. It can also provide you with valuable skills and experiences that you can apply to your future career. Here are some tips on how to volunteer or intern in the community during your study abroad program:

1. Research local organizations:

Before you arrive in your host country, research local organizations that align with your interests and skills. Look for opportunities to volunteer or intern with organizations that work on issues you care about.

2. **Attend a study abroad orientation:**

Many study abroad programs offer an orientation session where you can learn about volunteer and internship opportunities. Attend this session to get a better understanding of what's available and how to get involved.

3. **Reach out to local organizations:**

Once you arrive in your host country, reach out to local organizations that interest you. Send an email or make a phone call to inquire about volunteer or internship opportunities.

4. **Network:**

Use your study abroad program to network and make connections in the local community. Attend events and conferences related to your field of interest and meet new people who can provide valuable advice and guidance

5 Be flexible:

Volunteering or interning in a new country can be challenging, and things may not always go according to plan.

Be flexible and open to new experiences and learning opportunities.

6. Learn from the experience:

Take the time to reflect on your volunteer or internship experience and what you have learned. This can be a great opportunity to gain new skills and experiences that can be applied to your future career.

7. Document your experience:

Take pictures, write a journal, or create a blog to document your volunteer or internship experience. This can be a great way to share your experience with others and reflect on what you have learned.

In conclusion, volunteering or interning in the local community during your study abroad program can be a valuable experience that allows you to give back and gain new skills and experiences. Research local organizations, attend a study abroad orientation, reach out to local organizations, network, be flexible, learn from the experience, and document your experience. With these tips, you can make the most of your study abroad program and make a positive impact in the local community.

D. Participating in cultural events and festivals

Participating in cultural events and festivals during your study abroad program is an excellent way to learn about the local culture, meet new people, and create unforgettable memories. Here are some tips on how to make the most of cultural events and festivals during your study abroad program:

1. Research upcoming events:
Before you arrive in your host country, research upcoming cultural events and festivals. Look for events that align with your interests and schedule.

2. Attend the study abroad orientation:
Many study abroad programs offer an orientation session where you can learn about cultural events and festivals. Attend this session to get a better understanding of what's available and how to participate.

3. Ask Locals:
Once you arrive in your host country, ask locals about upcoming cultural events and festivals. They may have recommendations for events that are not listed online.

4. Be Respectful:
When participating in cultural events and festivals, be respectful of the local culture and customs. Follow any dress codes or etiquette guidelines that may be in place.

5. Try new foods:
Food is an essential part of many cultural events and festivals. Be open to trying new foods and flavors, even if they are unfamiliar.

6. Participate in activities:

Cultural events and festivals often include activities and games that allow participants to learn about the local culture. Participate in these activities to gain a deeper understanding of the local traditions.

7. Document your experience:

Take pictures, write a journal, or create a blog to document your experience at cultural events and festivals. This can be a great way to share your experience with others and reflect on what you have learned.

In conclusion, participating in cultural events and festivals during your study abroad program can be an enriching experience that allows you to learn about the local culture, meet new people, and create unforgettable memories. Research upcoming events, attend the study abroad orientation, ask locals, be respectful, try new foods, participate in activities, and document your experience. With these tips, you can make the most of your study abroad program and gain a deeper understanding of the local culture.

E. Planning travel excursions

Planning travel excursions during your study abroad program can be a great way to explore new places, meet new people, and create unforgettable memories. However, it can also be overwhelming and stressful, especially if you are unfamiliar with the local area. Here are some tips on how to plan travel excursions during your study abroad program:

1. **Research destinations:**
Before you start planning your travel excursions, research destinations that interest you. Look for places that align with your interests and budget.

2. **Create a budget:**
Create a budget for your travel excursions and stick to it. Consider the cost of transportation, accommodation, food, and activities when creating your budget.

3. **Plan ahead:**
Plan your travel excursions in advance to avoid last-minute stress and unexpected expenses. Consider the time of year, weather, and any holidays or events that may impact your travel plans.

4. **Use travel resources:**
Use travel resources such as guidBooks, travel websites, and travel blogs to research destinations, find accommodation, and plan activities.

5. **Consider group travel:**
Group travel can be a great way to save money and meet new people. Consider joining a group tour or organizing a trip with other students in your study abroad program.

6.**Be flexible:** Travel plans may change due to unforeseen circumstances, such as weather or transportation delays. Be flexible and have a backup plan in case things don't go according to plan.

7.**Stay safe:** When planning travel excursions, prioritize your safety. Research local laws and customs, and take necessary precautions to avoid dangerous situations.

In conclusion, planning travel excursions during your study abroad program can be a rewarding experience that allows you to explore new places, meet new people, and create unforgettable memories. Research destinations, create a budget, plan ahead, use travel resources, consider group travel, be flexible, and stay safe. With these tips, you can make the most of your study abroad program and explore new places with confidence.

Career Benefits of Studying Abroad After 12th

A. Gaining international experience and cultural competency

Studying abroad is an excellent way to gain international experience and cultural competency. It allows students to immerse themselves in a new culture, gain a better understanding of global issues, and develop intercultural communication skills. Here are some ways to gain international experience and cultural competency during your study abroad program:

1. **Immerse yourself in the local culture:**
Make an effort to immerse yourself in the local culture by trying local foods, participating in cultural events, and learning about local traditions.

2. **Learn the language:**
Learning the local language can be a great way to gain cultural competency and connect with locals. Take language classes or practice speaking with locals.

3. **Participate in a homestay:**
Living with a local family can be a great way to gain cultural competency and experience daily life in a new culture.

4. **Take courses that focus on cultural competency:**
Choose courses that focus on global issues, intercultural communication, or other topics that relate to cultural competency.

5. Volunteer or intern in the local community:
Volunteering or interning in the local community can be a great way to gain international experience and cultural competency while also making a positive impact.

6. **Travel and explore:**
Take advantage of your time abroad to travel and explore new places. This can be a great way to gain a broader perspective on global issues and gain a better understanding of different cultures.

7. **Reflect on your experience:**
Take time to reflect on your experiences and what you have learned. This can be a great way to process your experiences and gain a deeper understanding of the local culture.

In conclusion, studying abroad is an excellent way to gain international experience and cultural competency. Immerse yourself in the local culture, learn the language, participate in a homestay, take courses that focus on cultural competency, volunteer or intern in the local community, travel and explore, and reflect on your experience. With these tips, you can make the most of your study abroad program and gain valuable skills and experiences that will benefit you throughout your personal and professional life.

B. Developing language skills

Studying abroad can be a great opportunity to develop language skills, especially if you are studying in a country where the native language is different from your own. Here are some ways to develop your language skills during your study abroad program:

1. Take language courses:

Taking language courses at a local university or language school can be a great way to improve your language skills. This will provide you with a structured and focused approach to learning the language.

2. Practice with locals:

Practicing with locals is an effective way to improve your language skills. This can be done by participating in language exchanges, attending conversation groups, or simply striking up a conversation with locals.

3. Immerse yourself in the language:

Immerse yourself in the language by listening to music, watching TV shows or movies, and reading books or newspapers in the target language.

4. Use language learning apps:

There are many language learning apps available that can help you practice your language skills on the go. Some popular options include Duolingo, Babbel, and Rosetta Stone.

5. Attend cultural events:

Attending cultural events, such as festivals or concerts, can be a great way to practice your language skills while also learning about the local culture.

6. **Keep a language journal:** Keeping a language journal can be a great way to track your progress and practice your writing skills. Write about your experiences in the target language and try to use new vocabulary and grammar structures.

7. **Don't be afraid to make mistakes:**
Learning a new language can be intimidating, and making mistakes is a natural part of the learning process. Don't be afraid to make mistakes and embrace them as opportunities for learning and growth.

In conclusion, studying abroad is an excellent way to develop language skills. Take language courses, practice with locals, immerse yourself in the language, use language learning apps, attend cultural events, keep a language journal, and don't be afraid to make mistakes. With these tips, you can make the most of your study abroad program and improve your language skills in a meaningful way.

C. Enhancing your resume and job prospects

Studying abroad can be a valuable experience that not only broadens your personal horizons but also enhances your resume and job prospects. Here are some ways to make the most of your study abroad program and boost your professional credentials:

1. Develop intercultural communication skills:

Studying abroad provides a unique opportunity to interact with people from different backgrounds and cultures. This can help you develop intercultural communication skills, which are highly valued by employers in today's global job market.

2. Gain language proficiency:

Learning a new language is a highly marketable skill that can set you apart from other job candidates. Use your study abroad program to improve your language proficiency by taking language classes, practicing with locals, and immersing yourself in the local culture.

3. Build a global network:

Studying abroad allows you to meet people from all over the world and build a global network. Stay in touch with your international contacts and leverage your network when applying for jobs or seeking career opportunities abroad.

4. Participate in internships or volunteer work:

Participating in internships or volunteer work during your study abroad program can provide you with valuable professional experience and demonstrate your commitment to making a positive impact in the world.

5. Take relevant coursework:

Choose courses that are relevant to your career goals or that demonstrate your willingness to learn about global issues. For example, if you are interested in a career in international development, take courses on global health, sustainability, or social entrepreneurship.

6. Highlight your study abroad experience on your resume:

Be sure to highlight your study abroad experience on your resume and emphasize the skills you developed while abroad. This can make you stand out to potential employers and demonstrate your commitment to personal and professional growth.

In conclusion, studying abroad can be a valuable experience that enhances your resume and job prospects. Develop intercultural communication skills, gain language proficiency, build a global network, participate in internships or volunteer work, take relevant coursework, and highlight your study abroad experience on your resume. With these tips, you can make the most of your study abroad program and boost your professional credentials.

D. Building a global professional network

Studying abroad provides a unique opportunity to build a global professional network, which can be a valuable asset in today's global job market. Here are some ways to build a global professional network during your study abroad program:

1. Attend career fairs:

Attend career fairs hosted by your study abroad program, the local university, or professional associations in your field. This is a great way to meet potential employers and learn about job opportunities in the local market.

2. Join professional associations:

Join professional associations in your field and attend local chapter events. This can help you build connections with professionals in your industry and stay up-to-date on the latest trends and developments.

3. Participate in networking events:

Attend networking events hosted by your study abroad program, the local university, or other professional organizations. This is a great way to meet new people, exchange ideas, and build relationships that could lead to future career opportunities.

4. Connect with alumni:

Connect with alumni of your study abroad program or the local university. They can provide valuable insight into the local job market, offer advice, and introduce you to other professionals in your field.

5. Volunteer or intern:

Volunteering or interning with a local organization or company can provide you with valuable professional experience and allow you to make connections with professionals in your field.

7. **Stay in touch:**

Stay in touch with the people you meet during your study abroad program by sending follow-up emails, connecting on social media, and attending alumni events. This can help you maintain and strengthen your professional connections over time.

In conclusion, building a global professional network during your study abroad program can be a valuable asset in today's global job market. Attend career fairs, join professional associations, participate in networking events, connect with alumni, volunteer or intern, use social media, and stay in touch with your connections. With these tips, you can make the most of your study abroad program and build a network that could lead to future career opportunities

E. Pursuing graduate study abroad opportunities

If you are considering pursuing graduate studies, studying abroad during your undergraduate program can be a great opportunity to explore graduate study abroad options. Here are some tips for pursuing graduate study abroad opportunities during your study abroad program:

1. Research graduate programs:

Research graduate programs in your field and determine which countries and universities offer programs that align with your interests and goals.

2. Consult with your academic advisor:

Consult with your academic advisor to ensure that the courses you take during your study abroad program will prepare you for graduate studies and meet the requirements of the programs you are considering.

3. Consider language requirements:

Some graduate programs may require proficiency in a particular language. Use your study abroad program to improve your language skills and consider taking language classes in preparation for graduate studies.

4. Network with professors and professionals:

Use your study abroad program to network with professors and professionals in your field. They can provide valuable insight into graduate programs and may be able to offer recommendations or connections.

5. Attend graduate school fairs:

Attend graduate school fairs hosted by your study abroad program or local universities. This is a great way to meet representatives from graduate programs and learn more about their offerings.

6. **Research funding opportunities:**

Research funding opportunities for graduate studies abroad, including scholarships, grants, and fellowships. Your study abroad program or academic advisor may be able to provide guidance on funding options.

7. **Plan ahead:**

Keep in mind that the application process for graduate programs abroad can be lengthy and require additional materials such as language proficiency exams or letters of recommendation. Plan ahead and start the application process early.

In conclusion, studying abroad during your undergraduate program can be a great opportunity to explore graduate study abroad options. Research graduate programs, consult with your academic advisor, consider language requirements, network with professors and professionals, attend graduate school fairs, research funding opportunities, and plan ahead. With these tips, you can make the most of your study abroad program and prepare for graduate studies abroad.

A. Overcoming culture shock

Studying abroad can be an exciting and life-changing experience, but it can also be challenging to adjust to a new culture. Culture shock is a common experience among study-abroad students, but there are ways to overcome it. Here are some tips for overcoming culture shock during your study abroad program:

1. **Learn about the culture:**

Research the culture of your host country before you leave and learn as much as you can about its customs, traditions, and social norms. This can help you understand and appreciate the differences you encounter.

2. **Embrace the differences:**

Instead of resisting or rejecting the differences you encounter, try to embrace them. This can help you appreciate the unique aspects of the culture and adapt more easily.

3. **Be open-minded:**

Be open-minded and flexible in your approach to new situations. Try to see things from the perspective of the locals and be willing to adapt your behavior to fit in with the culture.

4. **Build relationships:**

Build relationships with locals and other study-abroad students. This can help you feel more connected to the culture and provide opportunities to learn from others.

5. Stay connected to home:

While it's important to immerse yourself in the culture of your host country, it's also important to stay connected to your home culture. This can help you maintain a sense of balance and perspective.

6. Take care of yourself:
Culture shock can be stressful, so it's important to take care of yourself physically and emotionally. Eat well, exercise regularly, and take time to relax and recharge.

7. Seek support:
If you're struggling with culture shock, don't hesitate to seek support from your study abroad program, local resources, or other students. Talking to others who have experienced culture shock can be helpful and reassuring.

In conclusion, culture shock is a common experience among study abroad students, but it's possible to overcome it. Learn about the culture, embrace the differences, be open-minded, build relationships, stay connected to home, take care of yourself, and seek support. With these tips, you can navigate the challenges of studying abroad and enjoy a rich and rewarding cultural experience.

B. Adjusting to academic differences

Studying abroad can be an exciting opportunity to experience a different academic system and gain a new perspective on your field of study. However, adjusting to academic differences can be challenging. Here are some tips for adjusting to academic differences during your study abroad program:

1. Research the academic system:

Research the academic system of your host country before you leave. This can help you understand the expectations for coursework, exams, and class participation.

2. Consult with your academic advisor:

Consult with your academic advisor to ensure that the courses you take during your study abroad program will meet the requirements of your degree program and prepare you for future coursework.

3. **Communicate with your professors:**

Communicate with your professors and ask questions if you're unsure about expectations or requirements. They can provide valuable guidance and feedback.

4. **Adapt your study habits:**

Be prepared to adapt your study habits to fit the academic system of your host country. This may involve studying more independently, participating more in class discussions, or taking more exams.

5. **Seek academic support:** I

f you're struggling academically, don't hesitate to seek support from your study abroad program, local resources, or other students. They may be able to provide guidance or connect you with academic support services.

6 . **Manage your time:**
Time management is key to success in any academic system. Be sure to manage your time effectively and stay on top of coursework and assignments.

7. **Embrace the differences:**
Instead of resisting or rejecting the differences in the academic system, try to embrace them. This can help you appreciate the unique aspects of the academic culture and adapt more easily.

In conclusion, adjusting to academic differences during your study abroad program can be challenging, but it's possible to succeed with the right mindset and approach. Research the academic system, consult with your academic advisor, communicate with your professors, adapt your study habits, seek academic support, manage your time effectively, and embrace the differences. With these tips, you can make the most of your academic experience abroad and gain valuable skills and knowledge.

C. **Coping with academic and social pressures**

Studying abroad can be a thrilling and life-changing experience, but it can also come with academic and social pressures that can be overwhelming. Here are some tips for coping with academic and social pressures during your study abroad program:

1. **Manage your time:**

Effective time management is crucial for success in a study abroad program. Plan ahead, prioritize your responsibilities, and allocate your time wisely. Be sure to balance your academic and social commitments, and make time for self-care and relaxation.

2. **Seek academic support:**

If you're struggling academically, seek support from your professors, academic advisors, or other resources provided by your study abroad program. They can offer guidance, tutoring, or other academic support services.

3. **Join a support group:**

Many study abroad programs offer support groups or clubs where you can connect with other students and share your experiences. This can provide a sense of community and help alleviate feelings of isolation or homesickness.

4. **Take care of your mental and physical health:**

Prioritize self-care by eating healthy, getting enough sleep, and engaging in physical activity. Be sure to also take care of your mental health by seeking counseling services or other mental health resources if needed.

5. **Explore the local culture:**

Engage in local cultural activities to immerse yourself in the local culture and connect with the community. This can help you feel more at home and less isolated.

6. **Set realistic expectations:**

Recognize that studying abroad can be challenging, and it's normal to feel overwhelmed or anxious. Set realistic expectations for yourself and be patient with your progress.

7. **Connect with loved ones back home:**

Stay in touch with loved ones back home through social media, email, or video calls. This can provide a sense of comfort and support while you're away.

In conclusion, studying abroad can come with academic and social pressures, but with the right approach, you can cope with these challenges and have a successful and rewarding experience. Manage your time effectively, seek academic support, join a support group, take care of your mental and physical health, explore the local culture, set realistic expectations, and connect with loved ones back home. By taking these steps, you can overcome the pressures of studying abroad and make the most of your experience.

D. Dealing with homesickness and isolation

Studying abroad can be an exciting and transformative experience, but it can also be challenging, especially when it comes to dealing with homesickness and isolation. Here are some tips for coping with these feelings during your study abroad program:

1. **Acknowledge your feelings:**

It's important to acknowledge and accept your feelings of homesickness and isolation. It's normal to miss home and feel lonely in a new environment, but it's important to remember that these feelings are temporary and will pass with time.

2. **Stay connected with loved ones:**

Stay in touch with friends and family back home through regular phone calls, video chats, or emails. This can help you feel more connected and supported, even from a distance.

3. **Connect with others in your program:**

Participate in social activities and events organized by your study abroad program or join a club or organization. This can help you meet new people and make friends who are also experiencing the same feelings of homesickness and isolation.

4. **Explore the local area:**

Get out and explore the local area. This can help you get to know your new surroundings and find new places to enjoy. You might also find opportunities to connect with locals and make new friends.

5. **Practice self-care:**

Taking care of yourself is important when dealing with homesickness and isolation. This can include getting enough sleep, eating well, exercising regularly, and taking time to do things you enjoy.

6. **Keep a journal:**

Writing about your experiences can help you process your emotions and keep a record of your time abroad. It can also be a great way to reflect on your personal growth and development during your study abroad program.

7. **Seek support:**

If you're struggling with homesickness or isolation, reach out to the resources available through your study abroad program, such as a counselor or student support services. They can offer guidance and support to help you cope.

In conclusion, homesickness and isolation are common experiences during study abroad programs, but there are many strategies you can use to cope with these feelings. Acknowledge your feelings, stay connected with loved ones, connect with others in your program, explore the local area, practice self-care, keep a journal, and seek support if
needed. With time and effort, you can overcome homesickness and isolation and have a rewarding and fulfilling study abroad experience.

E. Addressing safety and security concerns

Studying abroad is an incredible opportunity to learn and grow, but it's important to address safety and security concerns during your program. Here are some tips to help ensure a safe and enjoyable study abroad experience:

1. **Research your destination:**

Before you depart for your study abroad program, do some research about the country or city you'll be visiting. Look for any travel advisories or safety warnings issued by your home country's government or by the host country's government.

2. **Know emergency contacts:**

Make sure you have emergency contacts saved in your phone and written down in case of an emergency. This should include the local emergency number, the embassy or consulate contact information for your home country, and the contact information for your program directors.

3. **Keep important documents safe:**

Keep copies of important documents, such as your passport, visa, and insurance information, in a secure location, and carry copies with you in case of an emergency.

4. **Be aware of your surroundings:**

Pay attention to your surroundings, and be cautious in unfamiliar areas. Avoid areas that are known for crime, especially at night, and stick to well-lit, populated areas.

5. **Stay connected with your program:**

Stay in regular contact with your study abroad program directors or advisors, and follow their safety guidelines and recommendations.

6. Stay informed about local events:

Keep informed about any upcoming events or protests that may affect your safety. Avoid large crowds or areas where protests are taking place.

7. Use transportation safely:

Use trusted transportation providers and be cautious when using public transportation, especially at night.

8. Follow local laws and customs:

Be respectful of local customs and laws, and be mindful of your behavior in public.

9. Take care of your health:

Make sure you're up-to-date on any necessary vaccinations or medical treatments, and take precautions to stay healthy, such as washing your hands regularly and avoiding unsafe food and water.

10. Have a plan for emergencies:

Know what to do in case of an emergency, such as a natural disaster or medical emergency. Keep a list of local hospitals or medical facilities, and know how to contact your program directors in case of an emergency.

In conclusion, addressing safety and security concerns during your study abroad program is crucial for a safe and enjoyable experience. Research your destination, know emergency contacts, keep important documents safe, be aware of your surroundings, stay connected with your program, stay informed about local events, use transportation safely, follow local laws and customs, take care of your health, and have a plan for emergencies. By taking these steps, you can help ensure a safe and rewarding study abroad experience.

Preparing for Re-Entry and Readjustment Back Home

A. Coping with reverse culture shock

Studying abroad can be a transformative experience, but many students face a new challenge upon their return home: reverse culture shock. This is the experience of feeling disoriented or disconnected from your home culture after spending an extended period of time in a different country. Here are some tips to help cope with reverse culture shock:

1. Acknowledge your feelings:

Recognize that feeling a sense of disorientation or frustration is a normal reaction to the experience of returning home. Allow yourself time to process your feelings and don't be too hard on yourself.

2. Stay in touch with your host culture:

Try to maintain connections with the people and culture of your host country. This can help you feel more connected and grounded, even while you're back in your home country.

3. Share your experiences:

Share your study abroad experiences with friends and family members. This can help you process your experiences and can also help others understand what you've been through.

4. Find a support network:

Seek out other students who have studied abroad or international students in your home country. They may be able to relate to your experiences and can offer support and understanding.

5. **Get involved in international activities:**

Join clubs or organizations that focus on international issues or cultures. This can help you stay connected to the global community and maintain your interest in other cultures.

6. **Keep an open mind:**

Try to keep an open mind about your home culture and be patient with the differences you may notice. Remember that you have changed and grown during your time abroad and that it's okay to see your home culture in a new light.

7. **Take action:**

Use the skills and knowledge you gained during your study abroad experience to make a positive impact in your home community. This can help you feel like you're still making a difference even though you're no longer abroad.

In conclusion, coping with reverse culture shock after a study abroad program can be a challenge, but it's important to remember that it's a normal experience. By acknowledging your feelings, staying connected to your host culture, finding support, getting involved in international activities, keeping an open mind, and taking action, you can help ease the transition back to your home country and continue to grow and learn from your study abroad experience.

B. Evaluating your study abroad experience

Studying abroad is an exciting and rewarding experience that can change your life in many ways. As your program comes to an end, it's important to take some time to evaluate your study abroad experience. Here are some tips to help you assess your time abroad:

1. Reflect on your goals:

Take some time to think about what you hoped to gain from your study abroad experience. Did you achieve your goals? Did you learn new things about yourself or the world around you? Write down your reflections in a journal or talk with a trusted friend or mentor.

2. Assess your academic performance:

Think about how you did academically while studying abroad. Did you find the coursework challenging or rewarding? Did you feel like you made progress in your field of study? Consider how your academic experience abroad may impact your future career goals.

3. Evaluate your cultural competency:

One of the most significant benefits of studying abroad is the opportunity to gain cultural competency. Think about how you adapted to a new culture and what you learned about the people and customs of your host country. Consider how this knowledge may impact your future personal and professional interactions.

4. Review your personal growth:

Studying abroad can be a transformative experience, both personally and professionally. Reflect on how you grew during your time abroad. Did you develop new skills or discover new interests? Did you gain a new perspective on your own culture or the world?

5. **Consider your future plans:**

Think about how your study abroad experience may impact your future plans. Do you plan to pursue a career that involves international work or travel? Are you interested in continuing your education abroad? Consider how you can use your study abroad experience to help achieve your future goals.

6. **Provide feedback to your study abroad program:**

Your feedback is valuable to your study abroad program. Let them know what worked well and what could be improved to help future students have a successful experience.

In conclusion, evaluating your study abroad experience is an important part of the process of studying abroad. By reflecting on your goals, assessing your academic performance, evaluating your cultural competency, reviewing your personal growth, considering your future plans, and providing feedback to your program, you can gain a better understanding of the impact your study abroad experience has had on you and how you can use this experience to shape your future.

C. Transferring credits back to your home institution

Studying abroad can be a valuable experience, but it's important to ensure that you receive academic credit for your coursework completed abroad. Here are some tips to help you transfer credits back to your home institution:

1. Start early:

It's important to start the credit transfer process early to ensure that you have enough time to complete all the necessary paperwork and meet all the requirements. Talk to your study abroad advisor and academic advisor at your home institution about the credit transfer process and deadlines.

2. Understand the requirements:

Each institution has different requirements for transferring credits from study abroad programs. Make sure you understand the requirements for your home institution and the study abroad program. Some institutions may require a minimum grade for credits to transfer, while others may require pre-approval for specific courses.

3. Keep track of your coursework:

Keep track of your coursework and syllabi from your study abroad program. You may need to provide this information to your home institution as part of the credit transfer process. It's also a good idea to keep a copy of your transcript from the study abroad program.

4. Meet with your academic advisor:

Meet with your academic advisor at your home institution to discuss how the credits will fit into your degree program. They can help you determine which courses will transfer and how they will count towards your degree requirements.

5. Submit paperwork on time:

Make sure to submit all the necessary paperwork on time. This may include a credit transfer form, syllabi, transcripts, and any other required documentation. Be sure to follow up with your home institution to ensure that your paperwork has been received and processed.

6. Keep copies of all paperwork:

Keep copies of all paperwork related to the credit transfer process, including emails and other correspondence. This can be helpful in case there are any issues with the credit transfer process.

In conclusion, transferring credits back to your home institution is an important part of the study abroad experience. By starting early, understanding the requirements, keeping track of your coursework, meeting with your academic advisor, submitting paperwork on time, and keeping copies of all paperwork, you can ensure that you receive academic credit for your study abroad program and stay on track towards graduation.

D. Identifying opportunities to share your experience

Studying abroad is a life-changing experience that offers many opportunities to learn, grow, and explore new cultures. Once you return from your study abroad program, you may want to share your experience with others. Here are some ways to identify opportunities to share your experience:

1. Talk to your study abroad advisor:

Your study abroad advisor can provide you with information about how to share your experience with others. They may have contacts with alumni associations, student organizations, or other groups that are interested in hearing about study-abroad experiences.

2. Connect with your university's study abroad office:

Your university's study abroad office may have events or programs that allow you to share your experience with others. These events may include study abroad fairs, information sessions, or panels.

3. Join a student organization:

Many universities have student organizations focused on international issues or cultural exchange. These organizations can be a great way to meet like-minded students and share your study abroad experience with others.

4. Volunteer in your community:

Consider volunteering in your community to share your experience with others. You can give presentations at local schools, community centers, or other organizations.

5. **Start a blog or vlog:**
Starting a blog or vlog can be a great way to share your study abroad experience with a wider audience. You can share your thoughts, experiences, and advice with others who are interested in studying abroad.

Attend conferences or events: Look for conferences or events focused on international education, study abroad, or cultural exchange. These events can provide opportunities to network with professionals in the field and share your experience with others.

In conclusion, there are many opportunities to share your study abroad experience with others. Whether it's through your university's study abroad office, a student organization, volunteering in your community, starting a blog or vlog, or attending conferences or events, sharing your experience can help inspire others to pursue their own study abroad opportunities and broaden their horizons.

E. Using your study abroad experience to further your career goals

Studying abroad can be a transformative experience that not only broadens your horizons but also enhances your career prospects. Here are some ways to use your study abroad experience to further your career goals:

1. **Highlight your international experience on your resume:**
Make sure to include your study abroad experience on your resume, highlighting the skills and competencies you developed while studying abroad, such as intercultural communication, adaptability, and problem-solving.

2. Network with professionals in your field:
While studying abroad, take advantage of opportunities to network with professionals in your field. Attend industry events, connect with alumni in your field, and seek out informational interviews to learn more about job opportunities and career paths.

3. **Develop language skills:**
If you studied abroad in a country where a different language is spoken, make sure to highlight your language skills on your resume. Language proficiency can be a valuable asset in many industries, particularly in today's global economy.

4. Consider internships or volunteer work:
While studying abroad, consider internships or volunteer work in your field of interest. These experiences can provide valuable hands-on experience and help you make connections in your industry.
Reflect on your study abroad experience: Reflect on your study abroad experience and how it has influenced your career goals.

Consider how your experience has shaped your interests, values, and professional aspirations.

5. Reflect on your study abroad experience:

Reflect on your study abroad experience and how it has influenced your career goals. Consider how your experience has shaped your interests, values, and professional aspirations.

6. Seek out study abroad scholarships and fellowships:

Many organizations offer scholarships and fellowships for students who have studied abroad. These opportunities can provide funding for further study, internships, or other career-related experiences.

In conclusion, studying abroad can provide many opportunities to enhance your career prospects. By highlighting your international experience on your resume, networking with professionals in your field, developing language skills, considering internships or volunteer work, reflecting on your study abroad experience, and seeking out study abroad scholarships and fellowships, you can use your study abroad experience to further your career goals and stand out in a competitive job market.

Conclusion

A. Recap of the Book

This book on study abroad covers a wide range of topics related to the study abroad experience, including finding suitable accommodation, getting familiar with the local area, exploring local landmarks and attractions, joining student clubs and organizations, volunteering or interning in the community, participating in cultural events and festivals, planning travel excursions, gaining international experience and cultural competency, developing language skills, enhancing your resume and job prospects, building a global professional network, pursuing graduate study abroad opportunities, overcoming culture shock, adjusting to academic differences, coping with academic and social pressures, dealing with homesickness and isolation, addressing safety and security concerns, coping with reverse culture shock, evaluating your study abroad experience, and transferring credits back to your home institution.

Each chapter offers valuable insights and practical tips for making the most of your study abroad experience, from preparing for your trip to reflecting on your experience after you return. Whether you are a first-time traveler or a seasoned globetrotter, the Book provides valuable advice for navigating the challenges and opportunities of studying abroad and using your experience to further your personal and professional growth.

B. Encouragement to pursue study abroad opportunities after 12th

Studying abroad is a unique and life-changing opportunity for students, especially those who have just completed their 12th standard.

It can broaden their horizons, provide new perspectives, and help them gain a global perspective on their academic and personal goals. There are many reasons why students should consider studying abroad after completing their 12th standard. Firstly, it allows them to experience a new culture, language, and way of life. It helps them to develop independence, adaptability, and cultural sensitivity, which are highly valued in today's globalized world.

Secondly, studying abroad can provide a chance to gain a world-class education and access to advanced facilities and technologies that may not be available in their home country. Many countries offer scholarships and financial assistance to international students, making it more affordable for them to pursue higher education abroad.

Moreover, studying abroad can also improve one's language skills, as it provides an opportunity to immerse oneself in a new language and practice it daily in real-life situations. This can give an added advantage when it comes to career opportunities, as employers often seek candidates with strong language skills.

Studying abroad can also help students build a global professional network, which can be beneficial in the long run. It provides them with opportunities to connect with international peers, professors, and professionals, which can lead to potential collaborations and job opportunities.

Finally, studying abroad is a valuable life experience that can help students grow personally and professionally. It can help them become more independent, adaptable, and open-minded, and expose them to new ideas, cultures, and perspectives. This can help students gain a broader understanding of the world and develop a deeper sense of self-awareness.

In conclusion, pursuing study abroad opportunities after completing 12th standard can be an excellent investment in one's personal and professional growth. It provides a unique opportunity to explore the world, gain new skills, and broaden one's horizons, making it a truly enriching experience.

C. Next steps to get started on your study abroad journey.

Studying abroad can be a life-changing experience, providing opportunities for personal growth, cultural immersion, and academic excellence. However, the process of getting started on your study abroad journey can be overwhelming. Here are some next steps to help you get started:

1. Research:

The first step in planning your study abroad journey is to research the available options. This includes the countries, universities, and programs that align with your academic and personal goals. Consider factors such as the cost of living, language barriers, and cultural differences when making your decision.

2. Consult with an Advisor:

Once you have a clear idea of your study abroad goals, schedule an appointment with your academic advisor or study abroad office. They can provide valuable information about the application process, financial aid options, and academic requirements.

3. Apply:

After selecting a study abroad program, submit your application as early as possible to ensure that you meet all deadlines. This includes submitting transcripts, essays, and other required documents.

4. Budget:

Studying abroad can be costly, so it is important to create a budget for your expenses, including tuition fees, travel costs, and living expenses. Look for scholarships and financial aid opportunities to help cover the costs of your study abroad experience.

5. Prepare:

Once you have been accepted into a program, start preparing for your journey by obtaining a passport, securing your visa, and booking your travel arrangements. Additionally, research the local culture, customs, and language to help you feel more comfortable and prepared for your arrival.

6. Stay Connected:

Before you depart, stay connected with your family, friends, and peers, and stay in touch while you are abroad. Utilize social media, email, and video chats to stay connected and share your experiences.

In conclusion, preparing for a study abroad journey can seem daunting, but by taking these next steps, you can successfully navigate the process. With careful planning, research, and preparation, you can have a life-changing experience that enhances your personal growth, academic achievement, and cultural awareness.

Now What ?

**Get started on your study abroad journey
with these steps:**

- Step 1: Register on the Study Metro Portal.
- Step 2: Search for your dream university or programs, and discover universities offering application fee waivers.
- Step 3: Create your Study Abroad Profile here.
- Step 4: Submit your application to your dream university.
- Step 5: Claim your cashback.
- Step 6: Invite your friends to join the portal and earn even more cashback.

Take action now and make your study abroad dream a reality!